THE BOOK OF

FUN

AN ILLUSTRATED HISTORY
OF HAVING A GOOD TIME

by Russ Frushtick
Illustrated by Sonny Ross

RUNNING PRESS
PHILADELPHIA

Running Press
Hachette Book Group
1290 Avenue of the Americas, New York, NY 10104
www.runningpress.com
@Running_Press

Printed in China

First Edition: June 2022

Published by Running Press, an imprint of Perseus Books, LLC, a subsidiary of Hachette Book Group, Inc. The Running Press name and logo is a trademark of the Hachette Book Group.

The Hachette Speakers Bureau provides a wide range of authors for speaking events. To find out more, go to www.hachettespeakersbureau.com or call (866) 376-6591.

The publisher is not responsible for websites (or their content) that are not owned by the publisher.

Print book cover and interior design by Rachel Peckman.

Library of Congress Control Number: 2021948247

ISBNs: 978-0-7624-8048-7 (hardcover), 978-0-7624-8049-4 (ebook)

RRD-S

10 9 8 7 6 5 4 3 2 1

Contents

Foreword

BY JUSTIN MCELROY, CO-CREATOR OF THE ADVENTURE ZONE

I'm a firm believer that our highest calling as a species is to have fun.

Sure, I know, everybody needs food. Water? Wild about the stuff, drink it all the time. And shelter—don't even get me started. But they're not . . . fun, are they?

Fun is the thing you have when all the boring stuff is out of the way. When all your needs are met and you're staring at an empty to-do list, do you seek more shelter? Do you find other liquids to imbibe? Nope. You just let yourself have fun. (Not to say imbibing certain liquids can't be *strongly correlated* with fun-having.)

There are few people who understand this as well as Russ Frushtick. From the moment I met Russ in the trenches of game journalism, he's either been playing a game, talking about playing a game, or giving me a hard time for being worse at a game than he is.

That's . . . every game, by the way. The guy is weirdly masterful with his hand-eye coordination. In a different era or with a few different life choices, Russ would have been a renowned fighter pilot or high-ranking assassin. Instead, he has resigned his thumbs to bossing around plumbers and hedgehogs. All for the best, probably—he'd look pretty weird in a ghillie suit. More importantly, he understands fun and games on an almost instinctual level, a gift that would be a real shame to waste.

When you talk to Russ about a game, especially one he hasn't played, he dials in on what you're saying. You can see it. If I try to throw out a hot take about *Spelunky*, Russ isn't content to let my great joke just land; he wants to challenge it. "How many times did you try to whip the monkey?" he'll ask and then wait in silence, arms folded. He's not a pedant or contrarian, he just takes the art of fun really seriously.

I'm certain you're about to learn a ton from Russ; I feel like I'm smarter about games every time I talk to the guy. But I'm even more certain that you're about to have a lot of fun on this whirlwind tour. And isn't that the most important thing?

—Justin McElroy

Welcome to the History of Fun

Growing up, I loved video games. My passion led to common parental refrains: "It's a waste of time," "This isn't going to help you in life," and "Don't you have homework to do?"

And yet, somehow, I managed to make a career out of covering the video game industry—most recently as a co-founder of the gaming website Polygon. Against all odds, I turned those hours of throwing myself at *Super Mario Bros. 3* into experience I could use in my day-to-day life as a reporter, editor, and critic. Sometimes, it seems, there can be a lot of value in wasting time, kicking back, and having a little fun.

It's not just video games either. Humanity has found wildly diverse ways to have a blast, from cutthroat board games to animatronic robots, from quasi-safe amusement parks to bizarre roadside attractions. There are unlikely sports (like Swedish Bunny Hopping), the world and art of cosplay, and a host of other pursuits we've dreamed up to entertain ourselves.

While we may know where these pastimes ended up, their origins may not be as well-known. Why, for example, do people in Buñol, Spain, hurl tomatoes at one another every year? And who had the bright idea to make a board game about bankrupting your friends? Who were the first game streamers, and how did they inspire a fish to play *Pokémon*?

In this book, I'll explore the origins of fun. Some of these pastimes, games, and traditions stretch back centuries, while others are just a few years old. But all of them have one thing in common: Somewhere, at some time, there was a parent who was 100 percent convinced that they were a massive waste of time. I'm here to prove otherwise.

—Russ Frushtick

BOARD GAMES

Excavating the Oldest Board Games

Dating back to at least 3100 BCE, Senet is one of the earliest board games known to man. It's played with two sets of pawns on a long, skinny board with three rows of boxes. Hieroglyphics from ancient Egypt portray all aspects of daily life, from prayer to war to killer bread recipes. There is even visual evidence of Egyptians' love of Senet, including Queen Nefertari kicking back while playing a game.

So how do you play? Well . . . bad news there: No one's really sure. The general consensus from board game experts is that the rules varied from place to place, but it probably bears some resemblance to Chess and Cribbage. Which means that, yes, Senet was also the first example of "house

rules," where whoever ran the game could dictate how it was played. So the next time Pharaoh tries to move two pawns in one turn, just take his word for it.

The Egyptians weren't content with just one game to while away their time by the Nile, though. Hounds and Jackals was created around 2000 BCE. It had an intricate game board with long pegs featuring the heads of, well, hounds and jackals carved into them. Historians assume it has similarities to modern Backgammon, with players racing to a point at the end of the board. Unfortunately, the official rules must have slipped behind an ancient couch cushion—this is another game we don't know exactly how to play.

Go and Chess

Thankfully, not all ancient board game rules have been lost to the sands of time. Go was created several thousand years ago in China (legends date it to around 2300 BCE) and is still actively played in its original form today. It may seem like a form of checkers, with white and black stones, but it's an enormously deep strategy game with an infinite number of variations. It's so complex that it took until the year 2015 CE for a computer AI to defeat a professional player at Go.

What we know as Chess was created in Persia around 600 CE. It was derived from an Indian game called Chaturanga (meaning "the four divisions"), referring to infantry, cavalry, chariotry, and elephantry. These would eventually morph into the pawns, knights, rooks, and bishops we know today.

Given its war-torn inspiration, it may come as no surprise that Chess has created a lot of conflict over the years. In 1026, King Canute the Great, ruler of the North Sea Empire, had a bit of a Chess spat with one of his Viking chieftains, Earl Ulf, when the king made a "false move" and demanded a do-over. Ulf was having none of it. Canute claimed that Ulf was a coward (something Vikings don't traditionally respond well to), and Ulf snapped back at him. Canute had Ulf killed the very next day . . . in church no less!

The Soviet Union was all too familiar with the dangers of Chess, especially in close quarters. In 1959, a Soviet scientist in Antarctica killed one of his compatriots with an axe after a disagreement over a game. Then, in the 1980s, the Soviet Union decided to ban its cosmonauts from playing Chess in space after a fistfight broke out over a Chess game.

Monopoly

The game we now know as Monopoly started as the Landlord's Game, created by Elizabeth Magie in 1904. Magie believed that the "value derived from land should belong equally to all members of society." In other words, "Sharing is caring." That's an amusing thought, given the cutthroat nature of Monopoly and the family turmoil it has launched over the years.

Perhaps appropriately, Magie's idea was stolen in 1932 by a man named Charles Darrow, who repackaged her game, renamed it Monopoly, and sold it to Parker Brothers, the world-famous board game maker, now known for games like Risk and Scrabble. In its first year shipping the game, Parker Brothers was selling 20,000 copies of Monopoly every week, making Darrow the first millionaire game designer (though we use the term *designer* very loosely here).

Elizabeth Magie's contribution to the history of board games wasn't uncovered until 1973, when an economics professor tried to sell a game called Anti-Monopoly. Parker Brothers sued him, but he countersued, eventually uncovering Magie's original patent from 1904. It wasn't until 1984 that Parker Brothers was able to earn the exclusive rights to sell Monopoly—though the rights did exclude the professor's Anti-Monopoly, a true win for the little guy.

THE GREAT MONOPOLY HEIST

In 1987, Monopoly partnered with McDonald's for a new promotion. When McDonald's customers purchased food, it came with Monopoly-themed stickers, representing the different properties on a corresponding game board. The stickers could be turned in for prizes, including cars and cash.

The promotion was so successful that it became an annual event, with the prizes increasing in value. To protect the integrity of the giveaway, McDonald's hired a security team to oversee the high-value stickers. The head of that security team, Jerome Jacobson, would go on to distribute the grand prize stickers to a network of criminals, who would end up winning nearly every major prize in the contest from 1995 to 2000.

Eventually, the scheme was uncovered, with 48 people pleading guilty to the scam. But it wasn't all bad: It was discovered that Jacobson sent a $1 million instant-win sticker to St. Jude's Children's Hospital in Tennessee, which McDonald's agreed to honor.

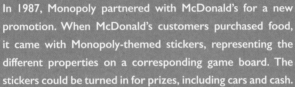

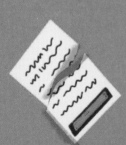

Dungeons & Dragons

In the early 1970s, Gary Gygax created a game called Chainmail, which simulated medieval combat with miniatures. In a twist, he added ways to adapt Chainmail's rules to a fantasy setting. Fellow games enthusiast Dave Arneson used these rules for his own dungeon exploration game, Blackmoor. Unlike most games of the time, in Blackmoor, players each controlled a single character.

Arneson and Gygax would soon join forces, gathering the successful elements from their various games and turning them into a super-game called Dungeons & Dragons. Gygax self-published the rules, selling copies for $10. Within a month, it had sold 150 copies. He couldn't keep up with demand, resulting in rampant piracy via photocopiers. Eventually, he found a publisher and began to sell D&D in stores as a more professional package that was slightly harder to illegally copy.

D&D has survived to this day and is now published by Wizards of the Coast. It has been cited in scientific studies for its positive influences on socialization and decision-making. See, half-orc assassins can be people, too!

SILLY CREATURES IN D&D HISTORY

When designing creatures for a game about the powers of the imagination, it's easy to get a little carried away. Here are a small handful of some of the weirdest critters to grace a D&D Monster Manual.

Gelatinous Cube (1974)

How do you make a Jell-O mold scary? Make it 5 meters tall and unstoppable. Unfortunately for the Cube, they're glacially slow, so maybe just don't go in that room and you'll be fine.

Flail Snail (1981)

Alright, so picture a normal snail. Now picture it bigger. Now, instead of a head, imagine it has four tentacles topped with slimy maces. Because . . . why not?

Stench Kow (1983)

It's a really smelly cow.

The Duck Bunny (1998)

The body, head, and ears of a rabbit with the bill and feet of a duck. GASP! While these fellows are hardly much of a threat, they are a good way to get a few laughs out of low-level adventurers.

Moon Rat (2003)

Normal rats are pretty smart, as animals go, but Moon Rats? Super geniuses . . . like smart enough to read scrolls and organize battle tactics. Impressive. Too bad it's only when the moon is full.

Catan

The man who revolutionized modern board games? A German dental technician, naturally. Miserable at work, Klaus Teuber found respite in creating his own board games, like Barbarossa, a clay-molding game that received critical praise. But he didn't hit it big until The Settlers of Catan (now simply named Catan), released in 1995.

Teuber was fascinated by the culture of the Icelandic Vikings, who colonized the island through cooperation and deception. Catan came out of this, with players trading resources like wool and bricks, building roads, and eventually, cities across a map surrounded by water. The game delved into how society would flourish or fail on an island with roads, robbers, and, yes, sheep.

The Settlers of Catan became such a hit that Teuber was able to retire from dentistry within three years of its release. The game has since gone on to become an international phenomenon, garnering fans like Facebook's founder, Mark Zuckerberg, and a handful of Green Bay Packers players who would gather for weekly games.

Catan has fictional fans, as well. The character Ben Wyatt on the TV show *Parks & Recreation* created the *Cones of Dunshire*, a parody of the board game. It was eventually made into its own, real-world board game, created by the same publisher behind *Catan*, Mayfair Games.

CATAN STARTING TO FEEL STALE?

Here's a selection of strange board games that will liven up your next dinner party.

The Campaign for North Africa (1979)

Each game is designed to take around 1,000 hours to complete. It's so detailed that it requires the Italian army to come with extra water rations so that they're able to boil pasta.

Unexploded Cow (2001)

In the 1990s, two issues faced Europe: mad cow disease in the UK and undetonated World War II bombs in France. This game tries to solve both at once, using the bombs to explode infected cows for fun and profit.

Pandemic (2008)

Eleven years before the appearance of COVID-19, a board game allowed players to save the world from four deadly diseases. Unlike most board games, it is entirely cooperative. It's just you and your friends against a gang of superbugs.

Nuns on the Run (2010)

Players take on the role of scheming nuns, sneaking around their abbey trying to collect items that are strictly on the no-no list: letters from lovers, books of dark magic, and even liquid opium. Great for fans of stealthy play who also love a little blasphemy.

King of Tokyo (2011)

Kings and queens have their place, but the only true rulers in this world? Giant monsters! Take command of mutant beasts, giant penguins, and cyber cats as they duke it out with laser vision and fire breath.

Ancient Toys

There's something ingrained in the human psyche that just makes us love toys. Sticks and rocks were some of the first playthings, and ancient Egyptian marbles were discovered in a child's grave from 4000 BCE.

The oldest constructed toys date back to the Indus Valley civilization, which began in 3300 BCE. Archaeologists have discovered toy carts and figurines, usually made from terra-cotta, depicting oxen pulling hay and grain. There were also monkey toys that could climb, with moving parts connected by string and attached with drilled holes.

MINI-KNIGHTS

During the Middle Ages, the hobby horse, a carved wooden horse head at the end of a stick, came into fashion. Hobby horse enthusiasts were often seen with scopperels—long sticks with pinwheels at the end. Kids would act out mock jousts, charging at one another while "riding" on their hobby horses with scopperels raised at chest height (this definitely ended well).

But it wasn't just kids risking life and limb for a little fun back then. An illustration dating back to the 1300s depicts a woman standing on stilts . . . while nursing a newborn baby. Thus far we've struggled to find any modern parenting books that encourage this sort of behavior, but, hey, whatever gets them to sleep, right?

How Dolls Evolved from Corn

While the earliest dolls were made of simple materials, like stone, wool, or even corn husks, over time they became increasingly complex and laden with meaning.

In Japan in 1625, members of the court would bring dolls for the emperor's daughter to play with. When she became Empress Meishō in 1687, the national holiday known as Hinamatsuri was born. On the holiday, also called Girls' Day or Dolls' Day, Japanese families display intricate dolls in a traditional wedding ceremony. While the dolls were originally meant to be playthings, they've since become decorative and ceremonial, which has to be tough to explain to youngsters across Japan.

CHINA DOLLS

In Germany, china dolls exploded in popularity in the 1800s and stayed ubiquitous into the 20th century. The name refers to the porcelain or "china" material used for the head and limbs. These were attached to a body made of cloth or leather. Demand for the dolls was high all over the world, with collectors willing to pay top dollar for these alabaster-skinned creations. They're still a good investment. In 2014, a one-off doll from manufacturer Kämmer & Reinhardt sold for a whopping $400,000, guaranteeing it would never be played with again.

The Rise of Barbie

Barbie remains the most famous doll ever made. Created by Ruth Handler, Barbie was inspired by Handler's daughter, Barbara, who would often play with paper dolls but would give them more adult professions. Dolls of the time usually depicted children and babies, but Handler saw promise in a doll based on an adult woman's figure. Her husband, a cofounder of the Mattel toy company, disagreed and rejected the idea.

Then, in 1956, Handler took a trip to Germany with her family and spotted a German doll called Bild Lilli with the proportions and backstory she had envisioned, complete with her own job and independent personality. Handler purchased three of the dolls, bringing them back to the US and redesigning them with the help of Mattel engineer Jack Ryan. The name, Barbie, came from her daughter, naturally.

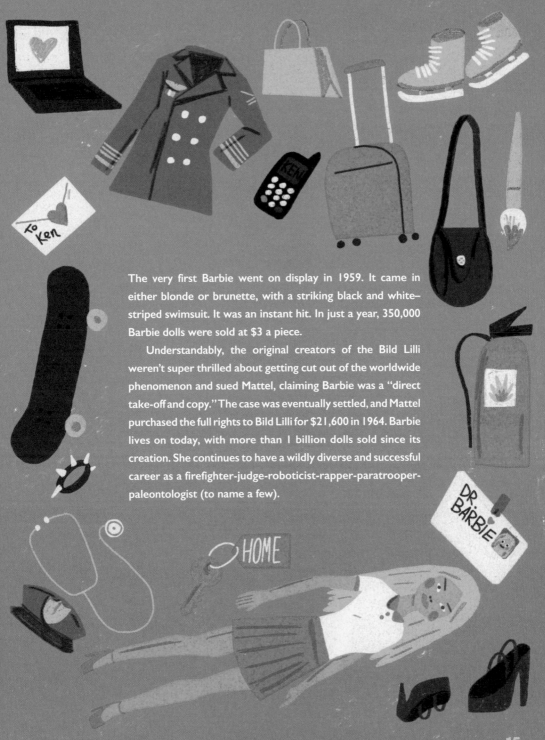

The very first Barbie went on display in 1959. It came in either blonde or brunette, with a striking black and white–striped swimsuit. It was an instant hit. In just a year, 350,000 Barbie dolls were sold at $3 a piece.

Understandably, the original creators of the Bild Lilli weren't super thrilled about getting cut out of the worldwide phenomenon and sued Mattel, claiming Barbie was a "direct take-off and copy." The case was eventually settled, and Mattel purchased the full rights to Bild Lilli for $21,600 in 1964. Barbie lives on today, with more than 1 billion dolls sold since its creation. She continues to have a wildly diverse and successful career as a firefighter-judge-roboticist-rapper-paratrooper-paleontologist (to name a few).

Rubik's Cube

Most toys are created with the intention of being, you know, fun. This cannot be said for the Rubik's Cube.

In 1974, Hungarian architect Ernő Rubik was working on a design tool in the shape of a cube, made up of parts that could move independently without it falling apart. After scrambling it a few times, he couldn't get it back to its starting position. He realized that he had a puzzle on his hands.

The "Magic Cube" was a hit at the Nuremberg Toy Fair in 1979. Unfortunately, "Magic Cube" was too generic to patent, so he renamed it after himself. While it's not the huge craze that it once was, the Rubik's Cube lives on, thanks to "SpeedCubing." The current record is a blistering 3.47 seconds, set by China's Yusheng Du in 2018.

The Slinky

In 1943, mechanical engineer Richard James was designing springs to keep naval equipment steady in rough seas. He accidentally knocked a spring off the shelf, where it gracefully "walked" down a stack of books to the table and then to the floor. Convinced that he had a hit toy on his hands, he fine-tuned the spring until it would "walk" with just a slight touch. His wife, Betty, named the toy "Slinky," after the dictionary definition: "graceful and sinuous."

James demonstrated his $1 Slinky at a department store, walking it down a ramp. Customers were captivated, and 400 Slinkys were sold in just 90 minutes. The Slinky has since become an institution both as a toy and as a scientific instrument. In 1985, NASA used Slinkys on the Space Shuttle to demonstrate the effects of microgravity. It did not go well for the Slinky. As Dr. Margaret Rhea Seddon, the astronaut in charge of the experiment, said, "It won't slink at all . . . it sort of droops."

From Teddy Bears to Beanie Babies

Stuffed animals hit it big in 1902 with the dawn of the teddy bear, created by Morris Michtom. The bear's name was inspired by then–US president Teddy Roosevelt, who was shown in a popular political cartoon sparing a helpless bear cub while on a hunt. Michtom sent Roosevelt one of his bears. The president loved it, granting him permission to use his name. The bears quickly became a worldwide phenomenon.

In 1980, Chicagoan H. Ty Warner was an aspiring actor, but after failing to find success, he went into his father's business, making and selling toys. Sadly, he was quickly fired. Despite being an incredibly good salesman, he had a reputation for selling his own toys rather than the company's. Unemployed, Warner went on a three-year trip to Italy. While there, he discovered a stuffed animal that used plastic beads instead of cotton as filler. Inspired, he came back to Chicago and founded Ty, Inc. His first hit beanbag toys were Himalayan cats—although his competitors thought they were a joke. "At first, everyone called them

roadkill and told me I was cheap," said Ty.

Ty launched Beanie Babies in 1994. There were nine different animals, including Pinches the Lobster and Legs the Frog. Ty's stroke of genius was "retiring" certain animals, as the retired Beanies became incredibly sought-after. One enterprising businesswoman found that she could buy Chilly the Polar Bears in Germany for just $7 a piece and then resell them in America for $1,800 each.

During the height of the craze, a divorcing couple was famously ordered to divide up their valuable Beanie Babies collection in the presence of a judge to ensure a fair split.

The very first stuffed animal was, ironically, a pincushion. The elephant-shaped sewing tool, made by Margarete Steiff in 1880, ended up being a hit with kids.

Early Building Blocks

While there have been records of simple alphabet blocks dating back to the 1500s, the concept of "building blocks" is relatively recent. R. L. and Maria Edgeworth referenced building blocks in their 1798 book, *Practical Education*. The idea was to teach kids the sciences through play. They proposed the idea of "rational toy-stores" that would sell building blocks and chemistry sets. While these sorts of toys would later flourish, the branding of "rational toy-stores" never did. Which is shocking. If there's one thing kids love, it's being rational!

In the mid-1800s, German educator Friedrich Froebel developed his "Froebel Gifts." These were different sets of blocks that became more complex as children aged, letting them create more detailed structures with wooden cubes, balls, and planks. Renowned American architect Frank Lloyd Wright credits his childhood Froebel set as being formative for his future career.

Wright's design for Tokyo's Imperial Hotel used interlocking log beams for stability during earthquakes. In 1917, his son John, also an architect, created a toy called "Lincoln Logs," a set of notched wooden pieces that could be used to build complex structures—or a simple wooden cabin.

Hello LEGO

Ole Kirk Christiansen was a failing carpenter working in Billund, Denmark. He never saw much success as a traditional carpenter, so in 1932 he tried his hand at making wooden toys, starting with a duck on wheels. He named his new company LEGO, from the Danish phrase *leg godt*, meaning "play well." The toys gained modest popularity and eventually he started turning a small profit . . . until his entire factory burned down.

Undaunted, Ole rebuilt the factory with the help of his son, Godtfred. In 1947, the pair discovered the popularity of Kiddicraft Self-Locking Bricks, first produced in the UK, and purchased a plastic mold to try to create their own. The locking mechanism was an improvement over simple stackable blocks, but early versions of the bricks lacked stability.

It wasn't until 1958 that the design for the modern LEGO brick was formalized and the bricks hit it big. Incredibly, the design hasn't changed since, and 1958 bricks will snap together perfectly with bricks made today.

The success of the plastic bricks couldn't have come at a better time: Yet another factory fire in

LEGO is the world's largest producer of rubber wheels, used on the various cars and trucks that appear in playsets. The company beats out car tire manufacturers with 870,000 wheels made every single day.

1960 torched any lingering wooden toy projects Ole had in the works, and LEGO became a plastic-toy company exclusively.

LEGO added a role-playing element with its first mini-figure in 1978, a police officer. These mini-figures have since become a staple of LEGO sets, ranging from race car drivers to pirates to a guy in a corn cob costume for some reason. They weren't without problems, though. The helmets on early astronaut mini-figures in the 1980s would frequently crack right on the chinstrap. *The LEGO Movie* (2014) poked fun at this with Benny the Spaceman, whose chinstrap was cracked in the same spot.

LEGO's success continues to this day, with movie franchises, video games, and collaborations keeping them current and in demand. But the building blocks of its business are still, well, building blocks. And the most complex set of them all? The *Star Wars* Millennium Falcon kit, released in 2017, which included 7,541 individual pieces. Certainly enough to fill an afternoon or two.

Toy Robots

The word *robot* as we know it wasn't really used until 1921, when it was coined by Czech sci-fi author Karel Čapek to describe the artificially created workers of his play *Rossum's Universal Robots*. Before that, the word *robota* in Czech just meant "forced labor" but had no sci-fi connection. The concept of "artificial workers" spread worldwide and, just a few years later, the first toy robots started appearing.

Mechanical toys, powered by steam or water, have existed since ancient times. Coming up with amusing "automata" was an important part of Leonardo da Vinci's day job of keeping princes and kings entertained. But the first recognizable "robot" toy, Lilliput, was created in Japan in the 1930s. Yellow and boxy, Lilliput didn't have much of a brain. All he could do was shamble slowly, thanks to a wind-up motor in his back. Not exactly the dark, machine-ruled future the Terminator would later warn us of.

The popularity of science fiction grew in the 1940s and '50s and ushered in the demand for more advanced toy robots. Robert the Robot, released in 1954, came with a wired remote control that let kids steer him forward and backward. Ads for Robert claimed he could perform a range of tasks, from delivering magazines to answering the telephone. They even claimed he could "look right through you with his X-Ray eyes." Fair to say, Robert wasn't capable of most of these tasks, but he did have a creepy voice box powered by a crank, proclaiming that he was "Robert Robot, the mechanical man." (We guess that counts as talking on the telephone?)

These early toy robots remained a huge hit with kids for decades.

Uh-Oh, They're Getting Smarter . . .

Thanks to the rise of computers and the popularity of the droids in *Star Wars*, the 1980s turned into a big decade for toy robots.

In 1985, toy maker Worlds of Wonder introduced Teddy Ruxpin, a teddy bear with a cassette tape player built into its chest. Teddy could interpret signals built into specially recorded cassettes, causing his mouth to move along with the words of the tape. Together with lullabies and even fire safety messages, the tapes revealed that Teddy wasn't a bear at all: He was an Illiop, an alien species from the fantasy planet of Grundo.

Other robots from the '80s include SkateBot (a skateboarding robot, natch) and Tomy's Dustbot, the first robot with a built-in vacuum cleaner.

The Furby Phenomenon

In 1998, Furby was, er, *hatched*, and the world went mad. Originally sold for $35, Furby was a furry, alien robot that could respond to voice commands and eventually speak in English if you talked to it enough. The maker, Tiger Electronics, didn't expect the demand to skyrocket that holiday season, causing resale Furby prices to hit hundreds of dollars.

Since then, no robot has quite hit Furby fame, though they remain a staple of toy stores, with *Star Wars* droids like R2D2 still ruling the robot roost. They've come a long way from their ancestor, Robert the Robot, with internet connectivity, gyroscopes, and video cameras.

23

Water Guns

The origin of the very first water pistol is still unknown, but there are references to them dating back to 1858. Students at Amherst College claim to have engaged in a "Squirt-Gun Riot," using it as a hazing tool for first-year students. In the book *Student Life at Amherst College*, one such gun is described as large, powerful, and "capable of drenching a Freshman at one fell squirt."

The first patented water gun was known as the "U.S.A. Liquid Pistol." Made of cast iron in the late 1800s, the small water gun was actually advertised as a self-defense tool. An early advertisement claimed the pistol would "stop the most vicious dog (or man) without permanent injury."

By 1934, the water gun went mass market. The sci-fi show *Buck Rogers* featured laser guns, and the design of the character's trusty sidearm was re-created with the XZ-44 Liquid Helium Toy Water Pistol.

After that, water guns didn't evolve much until 1989 with the dawn of the Super Soaker. Created by engineer Lonnie Johnson, it used air pressure from a hand-powered pump to ensure a powerful stream, changing the water gun wars forever.

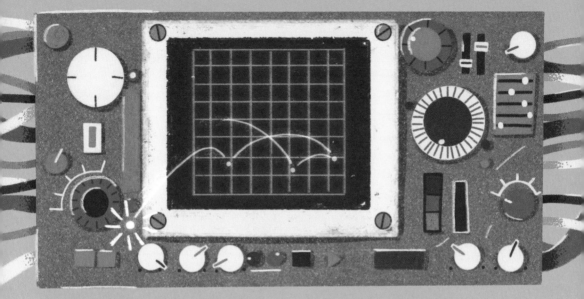

How Nuclear Power and Tennis Launched the Video Game Empire

In the 1950s, computer technology was on the rise, but the idea of using computers—then–room-sized monstrosities—for entertainment was an afterthought. They were mostly used for mathematical calculations that previously had to be done by hand. But as a way to demonstrate their power, a handful of simple interactive programs was designed.

The first game designed solely for entertainment was *Tennis for Two*. It was a tennis game created by American physicist William Higinbotham in 1958. Higinbotham worked in New York, at the Brookhaven National Laboratory, studying peaceful uses of nuclear power. But, once a year, the lab would open its doors to the public to demonstrate their work. Higinbotham found most of the demonstrations dull and static and opted for something more interesting to show the general public. *Tennis for Two* was a huge hit and hundreds lined up to play it.

Perhaps most incredible is just how advanced *Tennis for Two* is, considering its early origins. It features realistic tennis ball physics, with lobs, serves, and volleys represented by a bright white dot on a circular computer screen. If you look past the basic graphics, it has all the hallmarks of a modern tennis video game.

One of the earliest video games was a version of Tic-Tac-Toe where players had to use a rotary telephone controller to select which square they wanted. Not exactly thrilling.

The Great Video Game Crash of 1983

The early 1980s were a booming time for video games. Arcade games like *Pac-Man* and *Centipede*—a shooter game famous for its enormous, screen-crawling insect—were wildly popular. At the same time, the Atari 2600 became the first home game console with swappable cartridges, which meant it wasn't locked into playing a pre-loaded set of games. The success of the Atari 2600 led to increased competition from companies like ColecoVision and Intellivision, which made their own consoles and collections of games.

By 1983, the video game market was flooded. Game makers overestimated demand and produced way more games than audiences wanted. There was also the problem of quality: Game companies were rushing out poorly made knock-offs of popular games or movie tie-ins that no one wanted, like a truly awful *E.T.* game. There were no regulations to ensure that the games weren't piles of garbage. It was a cash grab, and it eventually came tumbling down.

Atari was hit the hardest. At its peak, the American company accounted for 80 percent of the video game market. But suddenly the biggest game maker in the world had countless unsold consoles and games taking up warehouse space. The solution: Bury it all in the desert! In September 1983, more than 10 tractor-trailer loads of game cartridges (an estimated 700,000) were driven to a desert outside Alamagordo, New Mexico, and buried. Local kids were said to have raided the pile in the weeks that followed.

While the Atari brand continues to survive to this day, the original company was a husk of itself by 1984.

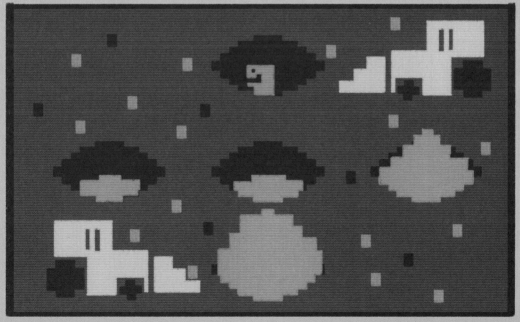

Nintendo to the Rescue

By 1985, the home video game industry had lost 97 percent of its revenue with the collapse of Atari. Meanwhile, Nintendo, a company out of Japan, had seen regional success with its Famicom game console and arcade games like *Mario Bros.* and *Donkey Kong*. Nintendo decided that Atari's worldwide downfall was its "rubbish games," according to then–company president Hiroshi Yamauchi, who saw an opportunity to fill the gap.

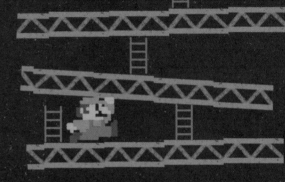

For the Famicom launch in the US in 1985, the company's console was renamed the Nintendo Entertainment System—they chose not to call it a "game system" so they could separate it from recently failed consoles. It even launched with a toy robot called R.O.B. to emphasize that it was

meant for kids and could be sold in toy stores. But perhaps most importantly, Nintendo's "Seal of Quality" limited the games that could be played on the NES to titles approved by the company itself. It was a guarantee to prevent the flood of knock-offs that doomed Atari. The strategy paid off, and 1.1 million NES consoles were sold in the US in the first year. Super Mario was suddenly a household name.

Mario's first appearance was in *Donkey Kong*. His name comes from a warehouse landlord named Mario Segale who loudly demanded rent from Nintendo's president while *Donkey Kong* was being developed.

The '90s Console Wars

After essentially reviving the video game industry in the late 1980s, Nintendo had full control over the market. Companies like Atari were mostly out of the picture, and the house that Mario built was at the top of the heap.

But another upstart out of Japan started making waves: Sega had released its own console, the Mega Drive, internationally called the Genesis.

The Genesis struggled to sell at first, packaged with a game called Altered Beast. But a new marketing team, based in America, decided to make a change, including a game called *Sonic the Hedgehog*. Sonic was massively popular with US audiences, and the Genesis managed to outsell the newly released Super Nintendo—the more powerful follow-up to the NES—in its first holiday season in 1991.

Sega aggressively targeted Nintendo in its advertisements, claiming "Genesis does what Nintendon't." These ads and the exclusivity of certain games, like Sonic and Mario, prompted an intense competition between owners of either console.

Unfortunately for Sega, it wasn't able to keep up the heat after the Genesis. Sony's PlayStation took over as Nintendo's main competitor in the late '90s. By 2001, Sega was forced to move away from making its own game consoles, sticking only to game development.

GoldenEye's Hospital Visit

Technological advances in the mid-1990s meant that games could mimic real life in ways that the blinking squares and circles of the '80s couldn't. But with that realism came concerns from parents that games were becoming too graphically violent and could be a bad influence on kids. To challenge that perception of violence in games, Nintendo billed itself as a family-friendly company. Nintendo games were often edited to ensure that they were appropriate for younger ages—for example, the blood was removed from the Super Nintendo version of *Mortal Kombat*.

But on the Nintendo 64, the company wanted to show that it could have more mature games as well. *GoldenEye 007* (1997) was a highly anticipated first-person shooter game that allowed players to control James Bond himself. But the original Mario creator, Shigeru Miyamoto, wasn't sure all this killing was right for the Nintendo audience. He came up with a solution, though! What if, at the end of the game, Bond could go to the hospital and shake hands with everyone he shot throughout the game? That way it could all end on a happy note!

Sadly, the hospital sequence never made the final cut. As a compromise, all the characters in the game were shown in the credits as "actors" of their various roles, making it clear that no one was really hurt. Close one!

How World of Warcraft Prepared Us for a Pandemic

In 2005, *World of Warcraft* had more than 5 million players hopping online to explore the fantasy lands of Azeroth. It was a perfectly re-created universe where people fought dragons, collected treasure, and rode mighty steeds. But there was more going on, too.

Part of the reason for *World of Warcraft*'s success was its social mechanics, allowing players to gather in massive virtual cities to chat together and trade goods. Surprisingly, this would end up helping researchers study the potential spread of a deadly virus, years before COVID-19.

One of the hardest bosses in the game, Hakkar the Soulflayer, was especially tricky because of the creature's "Corrupted Blood" spell. The spell would infect players with a disease, constantly draining their health points, while causing them to spread it to nearby players. The developers designed the disease to affect only players in a specific area, but they didn't take into account players' pets. Various animals could become asymptomatic carriers of the disease, bringing it back to major game cities to infect the low-level adventurers they'd run past.

It took a week for the bug to be fixed. In that span, players actively changed their habits, avoiding contact with major cities and crowds. Scientists have since used the event as a way to study real-world methods for disease outbreak control, using players' actions to determine how humans in the real world would deal with future pandemics (like COVID-19).

Unexpected Pokémon Go Consequences

On July 6, 2016, the world changed. Normally quiet parks and playgrounds were flooded with people staring down at their phones. Their goal? To catch 'em all.

Despite technical issues, the launch of *Pokémon Go* captured a massive audience of players, racking up 500 million downloads by the end of the year. The game's augmented-reality mechanics were unique, forcing people out of their homes to "find" *Pokémon* out in the real world. Upon discovering a *Pokémon*, players could toss virtual Pokéballs using their phone cameras, with the hope of snagging the adorable character.

This led to some pretty unexpected results. Shayla Wiggins, a 19-year-old in rural Wyoming, was exploring a river in her town, looking for water-type *Pokémon*. What she found was a dead body facedown in the river. Investigators declared it an accidental death, and while Wiggins was shaken at first, she later said she was thankful that she had helped find the body.

Not all of these explorations ended with a silver lining. A Bosnian organization had to issue a warning to players, encouraging them to not wander into minefields left over from the country's war in the mid-1990s. Not even a prized, shiny Squirtle is worth that risk.

The Birth of Game Streaming

Justin Kan started a website called Justin.tv in 2007. The site featured a live broadcast of Kan's life at all hours of the day and encouraged users to create their own broadcasts while participating in chats with the hosts. Within the first year, 30,000 broadcasters were streaming, and it quickly became clear that many of them were interested in streaming the video games they were playing. That meant the streamers didn't have to talk constantly to maintain the interest of the audience, and it made for more thrilling video than just someone in their basement talking into a webcam.

By June 2011, the demand for gaming broadcasts became so great that Justin.tv decided to split off its gaming category into a separate site: Twitch.tv. The offshoot quickly eclipsed the original, which was eventually shut down, leaving only Twitch. It only grew from there.

Twitch's popularity has led to some pretty unexpected moments. One of the best-known is "Twitch Plays *Pokémon*," a stream that had the chat room attempting to complete the original *Pokémon* Game Boy game by typing controls like UP and DOWN. These inputs were voted on by the chat room, which meant tens of thousands of people were attempting to control the game at once. Despite the resulting chaos, the game was completed in 16 nonstop days of streaming, with an average of 80,000 viewers at any one time. Shortly thereafter, a follow-up stream handed the *Pokémon* controls over to a fish for, yes, "Fish Plays *Pokémon*."

The Secrets of Video Game Development

You might think that video games are designed to follow very strict, predictable rules. But over the years, game designers have come up with subtle ways to make their games more fun, occasionally giving players an invisible edge. Here are some of our favorite secrets that designers have shared over the years.

Many platforming games, including the popular *Celeste*, have something called "coyote time." These games are programmed to make the player float in midair a split second after they leave a platform, so they don't instantly drop to their doom. The name comes from none other than Wile E. Coyote, noted defyer of gravity.

—Shared by *Celeste* designer Maddy Thorson

In *BioShock*, if you're facing away from an enemy like the enormous Big Daddy, they'll move just a bit slower so that you won't get smacked from behind as much.

—Shared by *BioShock* designer Jordan Thomas

In *Gears of War*, the developers found that players who didn't manage to get a kill in their first multiplayer match would quit without ever trying a second match. The solution? Give brand-new players huge advantages, like increased damage, that would slowly normalize after they've snagged a few kills.

—Shared by *Gears of War* designer Lee Perry

In *The Last of Us Part II*, the developers wanted the characters to catch their breath after doing a bit of sprinting. To pull this off, they programmed characters to have a virtual heartbeat. The more strenuous the activity, the faster the heart rate and the more they gasped for air. All the enemies you face have this same system, which means those marauders you're killing do, indeed, have a heart.

—Shared by *The Last of Us Part II* designer Anthony Newman

The designers of *Super Mario Bros.* wanted to have a second playable character, but technical limitations meant that it looked identical to the first player (Mario). All they could do was change the color of the second character . . . but the new color had to already exist in the game. The solution? Use the green of the Koopas for player 2's outfit. Thus, Luigi's preference for green was born.

—Shared by *Super Mario Bros.* designer Shigeru Miyamoto

THEME PARKS

The World's Oldest Amusement Park

In the year 1583, a Dane named Kirsten Pill discovered a natural spring about 10 kilometers outside of Copenhagen in a place called Dyrehavsbakken ("Deer Park's Hill"). At the time, clean drinking water was rare and the spring's fame brought crowds to the site. And what do crowds bring with them? Money! Entrepreneurial locals began selling food and water pots to the tourists. Inns flourished as weary travelers looked for places to stay.

The popularity of the spring took a hit, however, when in 1669 King Frederick III declared the land "royal hunting grounds" and banned the public from using the spring. It remained off-limits until 1756, when it was reopened by the old king's grandson.

Over time, more extravagant amusements have been added, like a wild animal park, cabarets, and clown shows. The popularity didn't even dip during the Napoleonic Wars, since people were hard up for some respite from the fighting. Incredibly, almost 500 years later, "Bakken" (as it's called by locals) is still going strong. It is known as the oldest amusement park in the world. It now hosts some modern attractions, like roller coasters and a "5-D" movie theater. And if you're feeling really brave, you can try drinking from the famous spring.

The First Roller Coasters

Roller coasters may be mainstays of amusement parks today, but that wasn't always the case. The first roller coasters were inspired by the "Russian Mountains" of the 17th century. These were hand-carved mountains of ice, designed for sledding, some of which were up to 80 feet tall.

Russian soldiers, occupying Paris in 1815 after Napoleon's defeat at Waterloo, are thought to have brought this hard-core sledding to France, inspiring what would be the first roller coaster. In 1817, a ride called Promenades Aeriennes ("Aerial Strolls") was introduced to the French public, featuring cars and a track but with the same basic idea as the Russian Mountains.

Things only escalated from there. The first looping roller coaster, "Loop-the-Loop," premiered in France in the 1850s. Unfortunately, the designers relied purely on centripetal force to keep the car attached to the track while it was upside down. This proved . . . unreliable. An accident during a test run shut down the effort.

These early looping roller coasters waned in popularity as Europeans looked for ways to entertain themselves that weren't so detrimental to their odds of staying alive. Soon, however, the Americans would revolutionize roller coasters and the amusement park industry with a little place known as Coney Island.

The Early Days of Coney Island

In the 1870s, Coney Island, located on the southern tip of Brooklyn, wasn't much more than a beach. But by 1880, all that changed. Developers saw potential in having fancy resorts within spitting distance of Manhattan.

The island's many new visitors were looking for more than just a day at the beach and a place to stay; they wanted an experience. In 1895, Sea Lion Park opened on Coney Island. Founded by Paul Boyton, the park hosted all sorts of rides and attractions, including the Flip Flap Railway, the first looping roller coaster in America, and Boyton's Water Chutes, a massive log flume ride.

One of these early resorts was the Elephant Hotel, an incredible 31-room hotel in the shape of a giant elephant. Until the Statue of Liberty was built in 1886, the Elephant Hotel was the first thing immigrants would see when sailing past Brooklyn, which is arguably a pretty exciting introduction to America.

Boyton was an eccentric showman, always looking for ways to bring attention to his park. He would frequently hold contests to see which animals could ride down his chutes. Reports indicate that the dancing bears were quite fond of it, whereas the baby elephants wanted nothing to do with it.

LUNA PARK AND THE CYCLONE

Boyton's Sea Lion Park only lasted for seven years, succumbing to competing parks. He sold his park in 1902 to Fredic Thompson and Elmer "Skip" Dundy, who had already seen success with a ride that simulated a trip to the moon. The pair called their new endeavor Luna Park (a reference to their popular ride).

Luna Park blew all other competitors out of the water. It was practically a city, built around a simulated lagoon and a 200-foot tower, with 50 buildings and 39 different shows. The park was lit with 250,000 lights when it opened, and 60,000 guests piled in for its first night.

The famous Cyclone roller coaster was built in 1927, right alongside Luna Park. The Cyclone was independently owned, which allowed it to survive as larger parks met their demise (the

original Luna Park shuttered in 1944). But it certainly went through hard times. In 1972, New York City was prepared to demolish it to make way for a new aquarium. Locals were concerned that the loss of such a storied ride would devastate Coney Island for good, launching the "Save the Cyclone" campaign.

The campaign worked, the coaster was saved, and the Cyclone became a New York City landmark in 1988, ensuring its long-term survival.

If you're looking to experience a bit of roller-coaster history for yourself, just know that the price for a ride is now $10 (up from 25 cents when it was first built) and that it can be a little, um, rough on the joints. The author lost his retainer on the ride in 1998, so please keep an eye out.

Disneyland's Opening Day Disaster

Disneyland opened in Anaheim, California, in 1955, and while it remains a signature staple of the world of amusement parks, it didn't exactly get off to a strong start.

It took more than 20 years of planning and $17 million for Disneyland to make it to opening day. The ABC television network broadcast the opening with a 90-minute live show hosted by future president Ronald Reagan. Everything was going great . . .

And then the doors opened to the public. The park was expecting 15,000 people on opening day and had preprinted invitations. However, those were quickly counterfeited and the fake tickets were sold, resulting in an attendance of nearly 30,000.

To make matters worse, the weather was unseasonably hot and a seven-mile line of cars formed on the highway leading into the park. Upon arriving, there weren't enough drinking fountains (thanks to a plumbers' strike), and the asphalt on Main Street, USA, melted, turning into a tar that caused visitors' shoes to get stuck.

A number of attractions (including Tomorrowland, which depicted what life would be like in futuristic 1986) weren't ready, and others malfunctioned. Mark Twain's riverboat almost sank after being filled to capacity.

Of course, Disney was able to triumph over some first-day jitters to become the juggernaut we know it as today. But nobody's perfect. In 2020, a Jungle Cruise boat sank in the middle of a ride at Disneyland's Florida offshoot, Disney World, forcing passengers to evacuate in spectacular fashion. Perhaps a bit of that first-day curse lives on.

The Republic of Children

What if children ran the world? That was the founding premise for this bizarre amusement park based in Argentina.

The Republic of Children was opened by President Juan Domingo Perón in 1951. The idea was to create a place where children could learn about the merits of democracy. The park features numerous world landmarks, like the Doge's Palace of Venice and the Taj Mahal, all shrunk down to child-size. It also has all the features of a major city, from an airport to theaters to hotels, all super small. Kids can even haggle over imaginary loans in a tiny bank. Whee!

Annually, children gather together in a little parliament, voting on laws that would affect the local region.

And this is all well and good. Children should learn about democracy, right? Unfortunately, Juan Domingo Perón was probably not the ideal teacher, having developed a reputation for censoring, imprisoning, and (for kicks!) torturing political adversaries.

The Republic of Children's popularity has ebbed and flowed over the course of Argentina's more politically tumultuous years, but today it remains an important reminder to kids that not all amusement parks are fun.

Sanrio Puroland

The Hello Kitty phenomenon has been going strong since 1974, but fans looking to fully immerse themselves in the universe of this mouthless white cat will have to travel to Tokyo's Sanrio Puroland.

Opened in 1990, the park is run by Sanrio (the creators of Hello Kitty and her friends). It features a wide range of attractions, like a mini-train that carries visitors around the park and the Sanrio Character Boat Ride, which is jammed with familiar faces like Keroppii the frog, Badtz-Maru the megalomaniacal penguin, and Gudetama the lazy sunny-side-up egg.

But the highlight of Sanrio Puroland is Lady Kitty House, where you can explore the world-famous cat's "actual" home. Apparently, she's a little self-absorbed, with paintings of her visage decking just about every wall. The tour ends with a photo of Kitty White herself. (Yes, her actual name is Kitty White. Calling her Hello Kitty to her face is a big sign of disrespect.)

Hello Kitty White is known for not having a mouth. Sanrio has given many explanations as to why, but the most recent is that she "speaks from the heart." Which is somehow both cute and creepy at the same time.

Soviet Bunker Park

The Soviet Union may be dead and gone, but tourists looking to relive the "glory days" of the Soviet regime still have a chance!

Based in Lithuania, the "amusement park" known as 1984: Survival Drama in a Soviet Bunker is built out of a legitimate Soviet bunker. Upon arriving, visitors are greeted by uniformed guards with German shepherds. The guards scream, "Welcome to the Soviet Union. Here you are nobody!"

What follows is a three-hour in-character experience where park-goers are treated to all the wonder and magic of Soviet rule, complete with pro-Communist anthems and dingy overcoats. Guards scream orders and march attendees through darkened bunker hallways before performing mock interrogations that end with signed "confessions."

In an interview with the *Guardian*, the creator of Soviet Bunker Park explained that it's not for everyone. "Someone always faints—our record is five people fainting in one show." She also mentioned that they have had to fire some of their "guards" for being a little too hard on the visitors. Some are actually former KGB agents.

The next time you complain about long lines at the cotton candy stand, remember, it could be worse.

The Park Built in a Nuclear Power Plant

Just left a ride feeling nauseous? It might be motion sickness . . . or it might be radiation poisoning!

Park-goers of Wunderland Kalkar in Germany will be treated to an unexpected sight as they approach the grounds: a nuclear cooling tower. That's because the park is built on the site of what once was an actual, functioning nuclear power plant. Why? Because the land was super cheap.

Back in 1985, the power plant known as SNR-300 was completed at a cost of just over $4 billion. At the time of its completion, political opposition to nuclear power was rising, and the local and federal governments were warring over whether to make this one operational. After some testing, it remained dormant for a year, at which point the Chernobyl disaster occurred. This didn't exactly get anyone super jazzed about flipping on the switch of this new plant.

By 1991, the unused plant was officially shuttered, with all the materials shipped off to various other plants. Many of the plant buildings were destroyed, except for the enormous cooling tower. Enter Dutch developer Hennie van der Most, who purchased the remnants of the facility for around $3 million. What a deal!

The new owner kept the cooling tower and turned the land into an amusement park, which he called Kernwasser Wunderland ("Nuclear Water Wonderland"). Apparently, the name freaked people out a bit too much, so it was renamed Wunderland Kalkar in 2005, after the local town.

As for the famous cooling tower? It houses a giant swing, a climbing wall, and, we've been assured, no radioactive materials.

The Gladiatorial Games

The first gladiators appeared at the funeral of a wealthy Roman citizen, Junius Brutus Pera, in 264 BCE. If a funeral seems like an odd place for a sword fight, consider that Pera's gladiators fought to the death, with the losers having the privilege of being their boss's attendant in the afterlife. It's arguably the worst silver medal in history.

Even though the gladiator battles started out as religious ceremonies, the Romans quickly realized that the spectacle of watching two men fight to the death could be used for entertainment. Advertisements were posted on Roman walls, proclaiming the names of the fighters and the days of the fight. Posters also listed the name of the person funding the fight, called the "giver." The giver of the fight would often enter their own slaves in the contest, forcing them to fight against their will. Not all gladiators were slaves, though, with some taking on the gig for the fame, glory, and money that came with it.

What began as smaller, one-on-one bouts with swords escalated to show the power and influence of the giver. The most intricate of these battles were called *Naumachaie* (Latin for "naval combat"), where sea battles were re-created inside of buildings. The Roman Colosseum was famously filled with water in 85 CE—with generous funding from Emperor Domitian—complete with warships and hundreds of unfortunate combatants. Water was redirected from the Tiber River using a series of aqueducts, giving the deadly affair a true sense of grandeur. Sitting in the splash zone was probably not encouraged.

Medieval Jousts

From the third century BCE to around 1400 CE, knights would frequently wear chain mail for protection. But there were drawbacks. Chain mail could protect a knight from a sword slice, but a lance to the chest would be a death sentence.

Advances in technology allowed the development of plate armor, made of solid pieces of metal, which gave knights much better protection (even if it made them less mobile). At the time, lances were used in warfare as a way for armored soldiers on horseback to "break a line," charging into a defensive position of enemy soldiers.

Medieval jousts were a re-creation of this tactic. Two knights on horseback would ride at one another with lances. The goal was to drive the point of one's lance into the shield or armor of the other knight. Thanks to the plate armor, these bouts were not meant to be fatal—though accidents did still happen. Their popularity made jousts incredibly lucrative as well. The fame that came with winning jousts allowed some commoner knights to earn titles and land, even if they weren't born into nobility.

The popularity of jousting as a sport came to an end in 1559, when King Henry II of France was wounded in the eye by a splintered lance and died of infection. It's all fun and games until someone kills the king.

Sumo Wrestling

Sumo is one of the world's oldest and still active organized sports, dating back more than 1,500 years. In Japanese, the word *sumo* means "mutual bruising," which seems appropriate, given the size of the combatants.

Sumo started out as a test of strength in combat but also has strong ties to the Shinto religion, and ceremonial traditions are still a major part of the sport today. Wrestlers throw salt, drink purified water, and stamp in the ring to ward off evil spirits. The prefight ceremonies usually take far longer than the fights themselves, which can be over in a matter of seconds.

Despite the pageantry of it, the rules are simple: If a sumo wrestler is pushed out of the ring or falls to the ground, they have lost. A wrestler can also lose if their loincloth manages to, well, drop off their person. This has happened only once, in May 2000, when a sumo named Asanokiri accidentally revealed himself to the crowd.

Winners are determined by a *gyoji*, a referee in religious garb. Gyoji take their jobs very seriously and actually come equipped with a ceremonial dagger, showing their willingness to kill themselves should they get a call wrong.

THE LIFE OF A SUMO WRESTLER

Successful sumo wrestlers can find fame and fortune, but it's far from an easy life. Think you can handle it? Here's a rundown of all the rules sumo wrestlers must follow, even when they're out of the ring.

1. Active sumo wrestlers are forced to live in a house with other wrestlers and can only move out if they quit sumo or get married. Junior wrestlers in the house do the chores for the more senior fighters and suffer relentless hazing rituals.

2. In addition to the minimalist wardrobe while fighting, wrestlers are forced to wear traditional Japanese clothes and maintain an Edo-period topknot hairstyle when in public.

3. Sumo wrestlers are not allowed to drive cars (perhaps a logistical consideration, given the small size of cars in Japan). They can, however, take mass transit.

4. Breakfast is banned from the sumo schedule. Instead, there is a large lunch, commonly made up of chankonabe, which is a hearty fish and meat stew, as well as beer. This is followed by a mandatory post-lunch nap. The regimen is intended to allow as much weight gain as possible.

Breaking any of the above rules can lead to fines and suspension from sumo wrestling. The dropout rates are, as you'd imagine, quite high.

Origins of Soccer

The earliest references to what we now know as soccer (or "football," as it's called in most parts of the world) date back to the third century BCE. A Chinese game called *cuju* was played with a leather ball stuffed with feathers. Teams of a dozen or more would try to kick the ball (hands were not allowed) into a single net in the center of the field.

Soccer's arrival in Europe was much later and far more violent. Early (and questionable) legends claim it began after an English battle, when soldiers took turns kicking the decapitated head of a Danish prince. It was definitely violent in the early days, earning the name "mob football," as rival neighborhoods' players would punch, kick, and gouge their way to victory. King Edward III of England would go on to ban soccer in 1365. In 1424, King James I of Scotland proclaimed in Parliament: "Na man play at the Fute-ball" ("No man shall play football").

It was eventually revived, though, and in 1815 modern soccer was split into two groups: Cambridge Rules, which prevented the use of hands, and Rugby Rules, which allowed carrying the ball (along with the preferred violence from days of yore). Cambridge Rules would be formalized with the creation of the Football Association in 1869, and thus modern soccer was born.

Cheese Rolling

Every year the small town of Brockworth, Gloucester, in England sees an influx of visitors. Rather than coming to see the historic St. George's Church (which dates back to 1142!), they come to hurl themselves down a hill while chasing a large wheel of cheese.

The Cooper's Hill Cheese Rolling is an annual event in Brockworth. The star of the show is a Double Gloucester round of cheese, which is rolled down Cooper's Hill, a notoriously steep slope in town. A large gaggle of people run after it, often tumbling wildly on the precarious surface in hopes of being the first to make it to the bottom of the hill, thereby winning the cheese.

The Cheese Roll's origins are up for debate, with a pagan fertility ritual as a possible inspiration. The first written mention of the event dates back to 1826, though that mention implies that it had been going on for far longer.

Injuries are common—and not just from falling down the slope but also from the cheese, which can reach speeds of 70 miles per hour as it barrels down the hill. In 2013, the 86-year-old cheese maker who provided the Double Gloucester was warned by police that she would be held liable for injuries.

Lucha Libre

In 1863, a Mexican wrestler named Enrique Ugatechea developed a new fighting style. Previously, wrestling was limited to strict Greco-Roman rules, where only a handful of "legal" moves were allowed and all the fighting had to be done with the upper body. Ugatechea's "freestyle" wrestling (*lucha libre* in Spanish) was far more flexible and exciting for spectators.

The most iconic aspect of Lucha Libre—the colorful, elaborate face mask—was originally established by an American wrestler, "Cyclone" Mackey (born Corbin James Massey), who always covered his face when wrestling in Mexico. The mystery of his identity made him extremely popular, and other masked wrestlers followed suit.

They're now known as *los enmascarados*.

Since then, masked wrestlers are considered the cream of the crop, with their identities closely guarded, reaching superhero status. One of the most famous, El Santo, was so cautious that he would even wear his mask in private. When traveling, he would book himself on separate flights so that his crewmates wouldn't see him maskless when he was going through security.

El Santo bid farewell to his fans in 1984, removing his mask in public for the first and only time of his career during a television interview shortly before his death. Afterwards, he was commemorated in his hometown with a large statue, complete with cape and, yes, his mask.

Kaiju Big Battel

New York City is home to a bizarre offshoot of professional wrestling known as "Kaiju Big Battel." Created by Rand and David Borden, Kaiju Big Battel shows feature live re-creations of giant monster battles, inspired by Japanese movie staples like Godzilla and Gamera, all within the confines of a ring.

Presiding over these battles is the Kaiju commissioner, described on the official website as "an enigmatic human-arbiter appointed by a clandestine cadre of world leaders to regulate Kaiju rage." (In reality, these are all just folks in goofy costumes, but go with it.)

The outrageous premises for the fights are often paired with current events. For example, during the height of the battle for health insurance in the US, one of the wrestlers, American Beetle, switched from Republican to Democrat so that he could afford an upcoming surgery with the support of Obamacare's better coverage.

Swedish Bunny Hopping

Horses may be known for their show jumping prowess, but there's another creature specifically designed for such a task—the mighty rabbit.

Originally popularized in Sweden in the 1970s, Kaninhoppning ("Bunny Hopping") features a variety of courses that rabbits (guided by their owners) must navigate, mostly by jumping. The courses vary from straight sprints to crooked switchbacks, some with high jumps, others with long jumps. Rabbits are judged on their ability to clear jumps without knocking over any of the railings in under two minutes. In the case of ties, completion time is also considered.

Since its humble beginnings, Bunny Hopping has become an internationally recognized sport, with clubs in Europe and the Americas.

Despite the sport's popularity, animal rights groups have taken issue with the use of leashes at Kaninhoppning events, though participants have a good excuse: Imagine what would happen if one of the critters got free. You ever try to catch a professional jumping rabbit?

The Windsor Pumpkin Regatta

Regattas, or boat races, date back to the 1700s and usually involve traditional wooden sailboats or rowboats. But not all of them.

The Windsor Pumpkin Regatta is an annual race held in Windsor, Nova Scotia. At a half-mile long, the distance isn't too intimidating until you realize what you'll be paddling: an enormous, hollowed-out pumpkin.

Thousands of spectators come to Windsor every year to see the best pumpkin racers in the world compete in a variety of events. The most thrilling of these is the motorized competition, where engines are slapped on the back of the large orange rides.

Climate change poses a huge threat to the Windsor Pumpkin Regatta. After 20 straight years, the 2019 competition was canceled when Hurricane Dorian spoiled the pumpkin harvest and rowers were without the 800-pound beastly pumpkins they needed to sustain their weight.

On the bright side, competing pumpkin regattas have started springing up across North America. This includes the West Coast Giant Pumpkin Regatta in Oregon, which proudly proclaims that its 1,000-pound giants are the true wonders of the aquatic pumpkin-racing world.

The Birth of the Daredevil

While circus performers were arguably the first daredevils, it wasn't until the 1800s that solo stunt daredevil acts, featuring death-defying feats, started to become popular. The first daredevil in America was Sam Patch, also known as the "Daring Yankee." As a child, he worked at a cotton mill in Rhode Island and would entertain the other child laborers by leaping off the mill's dam into the water below.

By the time Patch turned 20, his stunts had escalated and he began to draw larger crowds. In 1827, he amazed an audience by jumping down 70 feet off Paterson, New Jersey's Great Falls. The following year he jumped 130 feet off Niagara Falls in upstate New York. Adding to the spectacle of it, he would sometimes bring a bear cub on his jumps, trained to follow after him.

Patch's final jump was on November 13, 1828, in front of more than 10,000 fans. Unfortunately, a jump off Genesee Falls in Rochester, New York, went wrong and he landed badly on the water, never to resurface. Despite his short career, he became a folk hero in America, with plays and songs written about him. President Andrew Jackson even named his white horse Sam Patch after the one and only "Jersey Jumper."

Harry Houdini and the Art of Escape

In a traditional magic show, you might expect a few card tricks and maybe some sleight of hand. What you probably wouldn't expect is a man stripping naked while challenging police to handcuff him and lock him in a cell, only for him to escape. And yet that's how Harry Houdini became famous. Born in Hungary in 1874, Erik Weisz would become the most famous magician of all time—Harry Houdini. In his early magic career, rival magicians were never all that impressed by his sleight-of-hand skills. But Houdini did have another talent: the art of escape.

After achieving limited success as a typical magician, Houdini realized that his act needed a bit more showmanship. So, in 1900, he challenged the guards at Scotland Yard to lock him up, only for him to escape mysteriously. The feat earned him a steady performing gig at the Alhambra Theatre in London. As he gained fame, he would travel across Europe, challenging the local police to strip him naked, search him, and then lock him in a cell with shackles. He would escape shortly thereafter.

But as demand for his standard handcuff act trailed off, Houdini continued to escalate his performances. In another famous stunt, his milk-jug trick, he was shackled and placed inside a metal milk-jug can filled with water, only to break free minutes later.

This would progress to his "water torture cell," where Houdini was hung upside down in a glass tank by his ankles and shackled. Other risky stunts involved being locked inside a weighted crate and lowered into the East River of New York City (a health risk in and of itself). In 1915, he buried himself alive, without a casket, and was forced to dig his way out of his own grave, nearly suffocating in the process. What a showman!

Early Skydiving

The concept of jumping from great heights for no apparent reason is surprisingly old. Ancient Chinese legends speak of Emperor Shun who, around 2000 BCE, jumped off a tall roof to escape his murderous father. Shun *supposedly* used two large, cone-shaped hats to float to the ground safely. Please don't try this—it's a legend, after all.

Skydiving in Europe dates back to the Middle Ages, when intrepid adventurers would try to glide to safety after jumping from particularly high towers. One of the popular techniques, made famous by a man named Abbas ibn Firnas in 852 CE, involved donning a cloak with wooden struts (think Batman's cape). Firnas's cloak didn't allow him to take flight, but it did slow his descent enough that he wasn't killed outright.

More modern parachutes didn't arrive until the 1700s. Louis-Sébastien Lenormand of France developed an umbrella-like device that he used to survive a fall, eventually coining the term *parachute* (meaning "to avert a fall"). Just a few years later, in 1785, Jean-Pierre Blanchard used a parachute to "safely" eject a dog from a hot-air balloon. Blanchard would test it himself, though, when he was forced to bail out of a ruptured balloon in 1793. The parachute worked, and we've been using similar designs ever since.

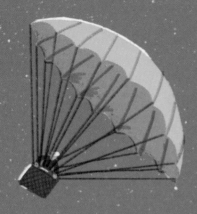

SKYDIVING FROM THE STRATOSPHERE

Once skydiving became a reality, it wasn't long before people started pushing the boundaries of what was possible.

In 1960, Colonel Joseph Kittinger of the US Air Force jumped from a balloon at 102,800 feet (more than 19 miles) above the earth. Project Excelsior, as it was called, was designed by the military to test the safety of bailing out of reconnaissance planes at high altitudes. It was a practical scientific experiment and was never intended to be a record-setting publicity stunt, but Kittinger's skydive would remain a record for 51 years.

In 2012, Felix Baumgartner, coached by Kittinger, broke the skydiving record, jumping from 127,852 feet. Baumgartner became the first person to break the sound barrier outside of a vehicle, reaching 843 miles per hour in his fall.

But unlike Kittinger, Baumgartner's record fall would be bested just two years later. Alan Eustace, an engineer at Google, took the top spot, falling from 135,890 feet. He was no passive participant, either, developing the spacesuit he would don for the jump. Speaking with *Business Insider* in 2019, Eustace said he never saw himself as a daredevil, though. "I kind of liked the idea of an old, ancient engineer setting a world record for skydiving."

The Father of Movie Stunts: Buster Keaton

In the early days of movies, there was little demand for non-acting stunt artists. Despite film stunts being tremendously risky, the stars of the films would often perform these stunts themselves, occasionally leading to injury or even death. While there were talented stunt actors before him, successful silent film star Buster Keaton's stunts remain some of the most complex and dangerous maneuvers ever captured on film.

In arguably his most famous stunt, from *Steamboat Bill, Jr.* (1928), Keaton stood in a specific spot during a cyclone scene as the entire front of a house fell all around him. The façade was real, weighing two tons, and would have crushed him instantly if anything went wrong. The only reason he avoided death was because of the precise placement of an upstairs window, which framed his body perfectly as it fell.

Other stunts had Keaton riding on the front of a speeding train or jumping off a moving car, all without camera tricks. He was so adept at these death-defying feats that he would often stand in for other actors in his films, acting as both star and stuntperson. In 1926's *The General*, Keaton crashed an entire locomotive into a river below, known to be the most expensive shot in the silent film era. (Obviously, there were no computer graphics back then—they actually crashed a whole train into a river!)

Keaton had an enormous impact on Hollywood, and his influence is still felt today, with everyone from Mel Brooks to Johnny Knoxville to Jackie Chan crediting his techniques and outrageous slapstick sense of humor as an inspiration for their work.

Helen Gibson

In the early 1900s, Helen Gibson found work as a fearless stunt rider for Wild West shows. Her skills developed, and in the early days of Hollywood, she performed in films like 1912's *Ranch Girls on a Rampage*, showing off her riding abilities (like being able to pick up a handkerchief from the ground while riding a horse at full gallop).

Her notoriety grew from there, and she soon graduated to starring in a series of 12-minute-long adventure films called *The Hazards of Helen*. In one scene, Gibson leapt from a rooftop onto a moving train, nearly falling off the side in the process. There was little in the way of safety equipment back then, so these stunts could easily have ended up with tragic results. It was a testament to the bravery of artists like Gibson, who were willing to risk their lives to get the shot.

In an era where women often played damsels in distress, Gibson was known for her strong, empowering roles, exhibiting courage in the face of danger. While she remains relatively unknown today, Gibson was a true pioneer for women in Hollywood and one of the most talented stunt-people in film history.

Annie Edson Taylor

Annie Edson Taylor was a widowed, 63-year-old schoolteacher in 1901. After the death of her husband, she traveled across the US and Mexico, trying to find work as a music instructor. But she was never able to make a steady living, so she decided to try something completely different: She would be the first person to ride off the side of Niagara Falls in a barrel. As you do.

A barrel, made of oak and iron, was designed specifically for the stunt. A mattress lined the inside so as to limit the damage to Edson Taylor during the tumble. In a test run of the barrel's structural stability, a cat was placed inside the barrel and made the fall with relatively minor injuries.

Now that it was her turn, Edson Taylor hopped into the barrel, which was then sealed and filled with compressed air. Her barrel then floated off the edge of Canadian Horseshoe Falls and plummeted 167 feet into the raging torrent below. Onlookers watched in horror as the barrel was quickly found and removed from the water. When the barrel was opened, Annie was fine, with just a small cut on her head.

Despite her plan, Annie Edson Taylor never made much money from the stunt, as the demand for her speaking tours quickly dried up. She did, however, find work selling souvenirs and taking photos with tourists by the Falls. She was eventually buried in a Niagara cemetery in an area known as "Stunter's Rest."

Jackie Chan Shouldn't Be Alive

Arguably the most famous stunt artist in the history of cinema, Jackie Chan placed himself in untold danger for his movies. Rather than using a stunt double, Chan opted to do almost all his stunts himself. Here are four of the stunts that nearly killed him.

Drunken Master (1978)

The original director quit the film when Chan said he wanted to crawl over hot coals during a crucial fight scene. Chan took over the direction and did the stunt as he envisioned, even shooting it twice for good measure.

Project A (1983)

Chan scripted a stunt that had him fall six stories through a handful of awnings before landing headfirst. Seems like a job for a stuntperson, but Chan did it himself, seriously injuring his spine in the process.

Armour of God (1986)

Chan had to leap onto a tree, pretend to lose his grip, and then fall to the ground. Easy, right? Unfortunately, Chan fell awkwardly, landing on his head, thereby fracturing his skull on some rocks. Whoops!

Super Cop (1992)

While hanging from a spinning bar in the middle of a fight, Chan was literally hit by a helicopter as it flew past the shot, breaking a rib and his shoulder in the process.

The Uninsurable Man: Evel Knievel

It wasn't easy for a man named Evel Knievel to get insurance, likely because his job involved jumping over large distances on a motorcycle. According to Knievel, famed insurance company Lloyd's of London turned him down 37 times when he asked for coverage. Probably a smart business move.

Knievel made a name for himself with his death-defying motorcycle jumps, but his success ratio was hardly perfect. When attempting to jump over the fountains in front of Caesar's Palace in Las Vegas in 1967, he came up short, breaking his pelvis, wrists, femur, and ankle in the process.

Despite the injury, Knievel continued jumping throughout the 1970s. While many jumps were successful, he continued to suffer countless injuries, recording 433 bone fractures over his career and earning himself a Guinness world record.

For his final major jump, he planned to leap over a tank of sharks on his motorcycle. But during a practice run, he ended up skidding off the track and crashed into a nearby cameraman, injuring both of them in the process. After a lifetime of horrendous injuries and risk, Knievel was ready to hang up his cape. While he never pulled off his final stunt, the television show *Happy Days* would memorialize it with Fonzie *successfully* jumping over a shark on his motorcycle, thereby birthing the term "jump the shark," for when a great show suffers a downturn and stages a publicity stunt to boost its ratings.

ROBBIE KNIEVEL JUMPS THE GRAND CANYON

Throughout Evel Knievel's career, he always talked about jumping the Grand Canyon on his motorcycle. Unfortunately, the US government would never grant him the air rights to cruise over the federally controlled land, so he never pulled it off.

His son, Robbie Knievel, decided that just wouldn't do.

A motorcycle daredevil in his own right, Robbie achieved fame by re-creating and occasionally landing some of his father's most famous failed stunts, including a Caesar's Palace jump that nearly killed his father. At least once, he managed to pull off what Evel could not, securing the rights to jump the Grand Canyon by using land owned by the native Hualapai Nation.

His 1999 jump was not clear across the canyon (which is more than 15 miles wide in places), but rather over one of the side gorges, at around 200 feet. Hitting the jump at 80 miles per hour, Robbie had plenty of speed and distance but landed awkwardly on the other side of the chasm. His bike spun out beneath him and he ended up careening into a safety wall set up at the end of the landing ramp, breaking his leg.

Like father, like son.

FESTIVALS

The Day of the Dead

Día de los Muertos, or the "Day of the Dead," originated in Mexico as a way to honor familial ancestors who had passed away. Despite the name, the festival actually takes place over multiple days, from October 31 to November 2. It dates back at least 500 years and is closely related to an Aztec festival that honored Mictēcacihuātl, their queen of the underworld.

During the 16th century, Spanish colonizers in Mexico witnessed the celebrations, which they viewed as blasphemous. Despite their violent attempts to erase the culture of the Aztec people, the beautiful tradition carries on today.

Rather than a somber affair, Día de los Muertos is an upbeat party where family members visit the graves of the departed, leaving their favorite snacks, toys, and photos to please the souls of the dead in makeshift altars called *ofrendas*. Poems called *calaveras literarias* ("skull poems") are read, often highlighting funny anecdotes and quirks about the dead. The poems can also mock living people with fake obituaries (usually for people currently in power) as a means of political satire.

Dances are held, as well. One of the most popular is the "Dance of the Little Old Men," where children dress up and move like elderly folks until a certain point in the song, when they spring up and really rock out.

Over the last 30 years, the tradition has risen in popularity throughout the Americas. It's also been heavily featured in pop culture, notably in video games (Grim Fandango) and movies (*Coco*), capturing the unique spectacle of the celebration for a new generation.

St. Patrick's Day

Ireland's best-known saint is Patrick. While most saints are considered sober reminders of a life piously lived, St. Patrick is now associated with, well, something else.

Born in the fourth century in Rome-controlled Britain, Patrick (according to his own "Declaration") was kidnapped by raiders and lived as a shepherd in Ireland before finding religion. He eventually escaped, became a priest, and returned to Ireland with the goal of converting the Druids to Christianity. Legend has it that he used the three-leafed shamrock as a way to explain Christianity's Holy Trinity to these Druids.

Over the years, his legend grew and he attained sainthood and eventually his very own day (March 17, the day of his death).

St. Patrick's Day is actually the most widespread national holiday in the world, celebrated by those of Irish descent the world over. While it has religious roots and ceremonies, it's best known as a day of celebrating Irish pride. And, despite taking place during Lent, the prohibition against alcohol is actually lifted by the church for the day. So the guy throwing up on your stoop is actually being quite pious.

In Chicago, the city's river is dyed neon green every year to celebrate St. Patrick's Day. The local plumbers' union is in charge of the task and uses 40 pounds of food coloring to achieve the perfect hue.

La Tomatina

If you find yourself in Buñol, Spain, on the last Wednesday in August, you may want to don a raincoat. The weather is fine there that time of year, but you're liable to get covered in tomatoes.

Every year, the small town of Buñol throws La Tomatina, arguably the largest annual food fight on the planet. The tradition began in the 1940s when an incidental scuffle during a parade knocked over a food cart, sending vegetables flying into the crowd. The aggrieved spectators nearby picked up the produce, started tossing it, and the festival was born.

It was, however, briefly banned in the 1950s due to concerns about property damage, but a protest march (featuring a coffin filled with tomatoes!) convinced the authorities that the festival should return.

If you do manage to visit Buñol, you should know that there are some rules to follow:

1. Tomatoes must be squashed before throwing.

2. Throwers must make way for trucks (apparently this is an issue).

3. The tomato throwing must stop at the sound of the alarm.

On the bright side, cleanup is pretty simple, thanks to the local fire department, whose members hose off the streets (and willing participants).

Spain's Baby-Jumping Festival

If you thought the annual tomato war of Buñol, Spain, was exciting, might we direct you to the tiny village of Castrillo de Murica? Every year the town hosts El Colacho, a festival that reenacts a true battle between good and evil.

The festival takes place in June and features local residents dressing up as devils while sprinting through the town, hurling insults at visitors and tourists. They've even got a traditional horsetail whip they can use to smack onlookers.

These devils have their fun for a bit, but eventually the sound of drums will herald the arrival of holy men who come to take these devils to task. And here's where the baby jumping comes in.

As the devils are being chased around by the pious drummers, they're led to a street filled with babies lying on mattresses, usually in groups of four. The devils will then leap over these rows of babies, all of whom were born within the last year. Town residents and festival-goers willingly offer up their newborns to be leapt over, believing that the close brush with satanic forces will exorcize any potential illness or bad luck from these babies in the coming years.

Once the devils have cleared the last batch of babies, they'll be chased out of town and won't reappear for another year. Reportedly, no babies have been injured in the process, but we also haven't seen their therapy bills.

The Origins of Carnival

For Christians, Lent is a time of holy and somber reflection, an abdication of vice in the six weeks leading up to Easter. It's not exactly "a blast." And thus came the demand for Carnival, a sort of last hurrah to do all the things you're not allowed to do during Lent.

Records of Carnival date back to the Middle Ages, but there's speculation that many of the traditions go back even further, to pre-Christian festivals like the Roman Saturnalia, which encouraged sex, gambling, and various other shenanigans.

Carnival continued these Roman traditions while reappropriating them as a Christian celebration focused on getting the sin out. And,

arguably, there's no better way to do that than to commit a ton of it. This new form of Carnival also allowed for a temporary measure of equality among the classes, as some slaves and peasants were permitted to openly mock the upper classes without fear of reprisal. Even today, colorful masks provide a level of anonymity, enabling people to really let their freak flags fly.

Of course, all this fun comes to an end right on Ash Wednesday with the start of Lent. It's a true challenge for those looking to jam in as much sin as possible in a short span of time.

CARNIVALS AROUND THE WORLD

Various celebrations of Carnival are staged all over the world, and each region has its own personal twist on the festival. The best-known Carnivals are in New Orleans (Mardi Gras, or "Fat Tuesday") and Rio de Janeiro. But those are far from the only places that celebrate. Here are some of the more interesting, and unique, Carnival festival traditions from all over the globe.

Russia: Maslenitsa ("Butter Week") takes place the week before Lent and encourages the mass consumption of dairy products. Pancakes, cheese, and crepes are especially popular.

Spain: Carnival in Catalonia is run by Sa Majestat el Rei Carnestoltes ("His Majesty King Carnival"), who oversees a variety of wacky activities, from bed races to a day dedicated to eating omelettes. Come Ash Wednesday, a funeral is held for the king.

Lithuania: On the night before Ash Wednesday, a choreographed battle is held between two characters, "porky" (representing winter) and "hempen man" (a stand-in for spring). The battle heralds the end of Carnival and the beginning of Lent.

Venezuela: Rather than a weeks-long affair, Carnival is just two days in Venezuela, at the beginning of March. During this time, kids are often seen hurling water balloons at unfortunate passersby.

Holi Festival

The Hindu celebration of spring, Holi, is one of the most upbeat festivals of the year for Indians. And yet its origins are surprisingly dark.

Legends state that Holi developed from a story about Prahlad, the son of a demon king. Prahlad had no love for his father (demon dad and all) and decided to kill him. But the king got wind of the plan and tossed Prahlad in a bonfire. The king's sister, Holika (the holiday's namesake), was instructed to hold the boy steady, utilizing a fireproof cloak to keep her from being burned. Spoiler alert: It didn't work. Prahlad was fine, Holika went up in smoke, and poof—good triumphs over evil.

The most striking part of Holi is the use of *gulal*, colored powder that festival-goers hurl at one another. Each of the colors represents a different aspect of the holiday, from fertility to the birth of spring. Heading out on the streets during Holi can be a little chaotic (don't wear your best suit), and it's a good idea to keep your skin and hair hydrated so you don't end up with a rainbow hairdo for a few weeks.

Chau Bun Festival

On the island of Cheung Chau in Hong Kong, a tower rises. While the skeleton of the tower is made of bamboo, the heart is all buns.

This is the Cheung Chau Bun Festival, which has been held annually for more than 200 years as a way to ward off evil spirits and pirates around the midsized fishing town. The festival features many familiar Chinese traditions, like dragon dances and parades, but the star of the show is at Pak Tai Temple, home of the Bun Towers.

There are three towers, each 60 feet tall, cov-

variety of delicious ingredients. Originally, large groups of young folks would try to scale the towers at once, but a tower collapse in 1978 meant the tradition had to be made safer.

Now only a select group of designated bun climbers challenge the towers by trying to snatch the highest buns they can, filling large white sacks to the brim with tasty treats. The higher they go, the more they ensure a better fortune for the coming year. And the winners? They're declared the King and Queen of the Buns, naturally. That's

Krampusnacht

Superman has his Lex Luthor, Batman has his Joker, and St. Nicholas has his Krampus. While St. Nick is known for his jolly disposition and penchant for giving presents to children, Krampus goes another way. This horned demon wanders the streets of Central Europe, punishing children who have been naughty.

The Feast of St. Nicholas takes place every year on December 6, but December 5 is all about Krampus. Krampusnacht ("Krampus Night") features large groups of adults dressing up as Krampus (horns, demon face, big wooly suit), while threatening children with sticks. It probably goes without saying, but there's usually a decent amount of alcohol consumed during the event. In fact, Krampus prefers a particular kind of fruity brandy, called Krampuslauf. It's worth keeping on hand if you're trying to stay on his good side.

Krampus has never had a lot of support from the Catholic Church, which views him as blasphemous. In Austria in the lead-up to World War II, Krampus was seen as a stand-in for communism (he is red, after all) and was banned outright. Despite all that, Krampus has survived throughout the generations and remains the edgy alternative to Santa Claus, making the holiday season just a little more interesting.

Icelandic Christmas

There is one gift that no Icelander can go without each Christmas season: new clothes. And it's not just because of the frigid temperatures, either. It's because of the Yule Cat.

According to Icelandic Christmas legend, those who aren't given new clothes are eaten by an enormous feline beast, the Yule Cat. The creature's origins are surprisingly capitalistic, though. Farm owners would reward their workers with new clothes upon finishing the annual wool harvest. Don't get the job done fast enough? Boom, you're cat food.

And it's not just the Yule Cat you have to worry about. There are also the Yule Lads: 13 demonic kids who wander through towns making mischief. Each is named after that lad's particular brand of mischief, including Spoon-Licker, Sausage-Swiper, and, uh, Doorway-Sniffer. Children who act up are threatened: Be nice or instead of presents on Christmas, you'll find a potato in your stocking, courtesy of the Lads.

As for the really bad kids, there's Gryla. This giant, the mother of the Yule Lads and the owner of the Yule Cat, emerges from her cave each year to hunt down misbehaving kids, whom she tosses into a sack and makes into a stew.

Are you still sure you want to make that trip to see the northern lights?

Finding a Home for Woodstock

The 1969 Woodstock Music Festival has since become a legendary moment in the history of music, featuring many of the greatest artists of the time. But it almost didn't happen because no one wanted to host it.

Originally, the festival was planned to take place in Wallkill, New York, with a promised attendance of no more than 50,000 people. The locals weren't particularly fond of the idea of hippies swarming the small town and pushed back, passing a law that required a permit for gatherings of more than 5,000 people. Woodstock was rejected and needed to find a new home.

Enter Max Yasgur, who was a leading dairy producer in upstate New York. Yasgur's Farm was home to 650 cows and had the space to support a 50,000-person festival. This made him unpopular with the locals, who posted signs saying, "Buy No Milk. Stop Max's Hippy Music Festival."

Despite the local opposition, the show went on and became the best-known music festival in history. It did, however, go a bit over initial estimates. Rather than the anticipated 50,000 attendees, Yasgur's Farm was swarmed by more than 400,000 people. Unfortunately, there is no record of how the cows felt about this.

Burning Man

In San Francisco in 1986, an artist named Larry Harvey built a nine-foot-tall wooden statue of a man. He took the statue to a local beach and burned it to celebrate the summer solstice. Happy with the results, he did the same thing the following year and the year after that. Each year the statue would get a bit bigger and more complex, and larger crowds would gather to watch it. By 1990, though, the police got wind of Harvey's annual bonfire and put a stop to the event.

Harvey needed to find a place to burn his statue in peace and joined a few friends from a local group called the Cacophony Society on a trip to the Black Rock Desert in northern Nevada. More than 350 people, many of whom had attended previous burnings of the statue, joined them. Out in the desert and finally permitted, Burning Man found its home.

Today Burning Man hosts more than 70,000 attendees and the Man has grown to over 80 feet tall. The organizers describe it as a temporary city, rather than a festival, with its own rules. It's home to bizarre art exhibitions, music performances, and even an Orgy Dome. Hey, what happens in the temporary city . . .

DRESSING UP

Deadly Masquerade Balls?

One of the earliest and most famous masquerade balls started off on the wrong foot. The year was 1393 and France's king Charles VI was celebrating the marriage of his queen's lady-in-waiting. The king, along with five of his court members, decided to dress up as wild woodmen, making costumes of grass and tar. (It should be noted that these costumes were fooling exactly no one.) This all would have been fine had the king's brother not brought a torch to the party. The king made it out alive, but four of the costumed patrons were burned alive. It has since become known as the Ball of the Burning Men.

Thankfully, not all masquerade balls have been quite so eventful. Their popularity skyrocketed in 16th-century Italy as a way to celebrate Venetian Carnival. The use of masks paired nicely with Carnival's tenets of social equality, anonymity, and debaucherous deeds.

And yet the hidden nature of guests' identities did prove unfortunate for another king in 1792, Gustav III of Sweden. The king had been warned that political assassins were planning a coup to be executed at an upcoming masquerade ball. During the ball, the king sat for 10 minutes in an exposed box and then proceeded to mock any potential assassins, saying that "this would have been an opportunity to shoot." Just moments later, the king was surrounded by masked men and shot in the back. Oops.

While large-scale masquerade balls remain rare today, intricate feathered Venetian masks and costumes remain fixtures at annual events like Mardi Gras . . . though hopefully they stay far away from open flames.

Clowns versus Kings:
A Battle for the Ages

Throughout history, clowns have played the important role of poking fun at social norms while also highlighting society's flaws. While the modern idea of a clown calls to mind a painted face and giant shoes, and (for some) evokes abject terror, the role has evolved throughout the centuries.

The earliest known clowns were court jesters, dating back to 2500 BCE. At the time, Pharaohs had jesters called *dangas* who would dress up in animal skins and masks to mimic and mock the Egyptian gods.

Ancient Greece had its own clowns, who would wear padded fat suits with comically large phalluses attached to the front and perform short shows onstage. Ancient Rome followed suit, developing multiple types of clowns. Some were dedicated to physical comedy and goofy faces while others offered parodies of more serious actors in the plays.

Throughout the Middle Ages, jesters were kept by powerful rulers for levity and were considered to be the only members in court who could openly mock the king. Kings were often surrounded by sycophants who would risk death for making even a simple joke about a royal, and a king who failed to take action against a prankster might appear as weak in his court. Jesters were given (mostly) free license to verbally abuse the king, sometimes becoming close confidants who were able to speak truth to power. There were limits, however. In 1535, Will Sommers, the jester of King Henry VIII of England, called Queen Anne "a ribald" (an older term for a crude person) and Princess Elizabeth "a bastard" after being challenged by a member of the court. The king made it clear that Sommers could be killed for such remarks, and Sommers made sure to be a little more careful with his words next time.

Gone Guising for Halloween

Halloween is thought to derive from the Celtic holiday of Samhain, which celebrated the end of the harvest festival and the start of winter. It was said that, during the two days of the festival, spirits were able to enter our world more easily, as the boundary between life and death was thinner then. Feasts and offerings were made to the spirits to appease them and ensure that livestock would survive the harsh winter.

Costumes have long been part of the celebration of Halloween. One example in Scotland dates back to 1585, where people would go door to door in disguise—a practice called "guising"—reciting songs and poems in exchange for food (an early example of trick-or-treating). The costumes they wore were meant to mimic the spirits who would visit the world of the living during this time, in an attempt to hide from them.

While dressing up for Halloween had become an established practice in Europe for centuries, it didn't arrive in North America until the early 1900s. It was around this time that Halloween was seen as more of a child's holiday (previously it was a time for adults to let loose and get tipsy).

HALLOWEEN TRENDS IN NORTH AMERICA

Popular costumes during Halloween are a surprisingly accurate reflection of cultural milestones, and the last 100 years have seen a wide range of different costumes, depending on what was happening in the world. Here are some of the more popular costume trends in North America and where they originated.

1910s

Wild West cowboys were all the rage due to western expansion and the popularity of Teddy Roosevelt, arguably the most cowboy-esque American president.

1930s

It took just a few years after the introduction of Disney's Mickey Mouse for his signature ears to become a staple of kids' costumes all over the US (and beyond).

1950s

Not exactly a time known for cultural sensitivity, the 1950s saw a spike in people dressing up in the native garb of people from around the world.

1960s and 1970s

During Watergate, political masks featuring Richard Nixon started popping up.

1990s

Power Rangers and *Pokémon* dominated the Halloween store shelves, bringing a newfound vibrancy to trick-or-treaters.

2000s

Thanks to the remarkably popular books (and the ease of getting a black cloak and a striped tie), Harry Potter characters spiked in the initial decade of the 21st century.

A Very Wet Ren Faire

The medieval age had a lot going for it, but alongside the cool knights and jousts were slightly less fun things like leprosy and the Black Death. Renaissance Fairs offered a chance to relive that magical time without risking a long, painful illness or death.

The 19th century saw increased fascination with the medieval era, with traditional-style jousts held throughout Europe. Their popularity reached a peak with the Eglinton Tournament of 1839, which hosted 100,000 spectators on Lord Eglinton's estate in southwest Scotland.

It . . . could have gone smoother. The plan was for 40 armored knights on horseback to march in a parade, picking up various ladies and officers at the stately home of Lord Eglinton before riding back within sight of the crowd that lined the lane. Horrible rain and overcrowding resulted in a gridlock of knights, totally soaked in their armor.

The tiltyard, set to host the traditional joust, was a muddy mess, and the grandstand's hand-painted roof started to leak. The day's joust was canceled, but the rains had also flooded nearby rivers, which meant that people in carriages were forced to walk through the mud to find food and shelter.

Eglinton continued the tournament two days later when the rains stopped, holding jousts and a medieval costume ball. But another freak rainstorm during the ball brought it to an early end.

The Three Types of War Reenactors

Civilizations have been re-creating classic battles since the ancient Romans (whose reenactments had their own body counts). The practice continues to this day, albeit under much safer circumstances. While ranks and other military structures are maintained during reenactments, there's another level of hierarchy that's helpful to know about when dealing with war reenactors.

"Farbs"

Casual reenactors who put as little effort as possible into their costumes or to staying in character. These are the folks who show up to a Civil War reenactment in sneakers. The term is thought to come from "far be it from authentic" or F.A.R.B.: "Forget About Research, Baby."

Mainstream

The middle ground of reenactors, these folks appear authentic to the untrained eye but don't necessarily obsess about the inner stitching of their costume and whether it matches period-appropriate sewing techniques.

Progressive

This group tries to mimic every aspect of the time period's dress, language, and culture as accurately as possible, with an emphasis on intense research. They're sometimes mocked as "stitch counters" or "stitch witches," a nod to their obsessiveness in attempting to match the exact number of stitches used in the original uniforms. Arguably not the kind of folks you want to have a beer with, unless it's mead.

Cosplay

While the term *cosplay* was invented relatively recently—in Japan in 1984—the practice of people dressing up as their favorite fictional characters has been around for far longer.

There's some debate over who would be considered the first cosplayers. One of the earliest recorded instances dates back to 1908, when a Cincinnati man named William Fell dressed as Mr. Skygack from Mars, an alien featured in a popular comic strip at the time. Skygack, it seems, was the Spider-Man of his day, and there are a number of reports of Skygack costumes appearing at various masked balls.

Conventions like Comic-Con are now tentpole events for cosplayers, but at the first science-fiction convention (1939's WorldCon), no one bothered to dress up. No one except Myrtle R. Douglas, who designed a pair of costumes for her and her partner, Forrest J. Ackerman. Douglas and Ackerman came dressed in futuristic outfits inspired by the 1936 H. G. Wells epic, *Things to Come*. A photo from the convention shows them proudly sporting shiny green outfits and capes, clearly shaming all others in attendance for their lack of commitment. Douglas (known as "Morojo" to the sci-fi community) is considered the mother of convention cosplay, inspiring generations to come.

THE GREATEST COSPLAY CROSSOVERS

As much fun as it is to come dressed as your favorite character, it can be a little disappointing to be the sixth Wonder Woman to walk through a convention hall. To stand out, cosplayers have had to get a little creative. Here are some of our favorite cosplay crossovers.

John Snow White

Transformers TARDIS

Jedi Wolverine

Iron Man Totoro

Django Fett Unchained

Steampunk Buzz Lightyear

Sub Zero Elsa

Sailor Pool

Minon R2D2

The Origins of Drag

Men have been dressing up and acting as women onstage for centuries. In Shakespeare's time, all the female roles were played by men, but the practice dates back as far as the ancient Greeks.

Drag is more than just men dressing up as women, though. Drag queen style is often over the top, splashy, and outrageous. Famous drag queen RuPaul is quoted as saying, "I do not impersonate females! How many women do you know who wear seven-inch heels, four-foot wigs, and skin-tight dresses?"

The first dedicated drag shows—known as drag balls—started in New York's Harlem in the 1920s and featured men playing women and vice versa. They were often attended by the gay and lesbian community and were held in secret, due to the risks of being outed at the time.

In the 1940s, a gay bar called Club Jewel Box hosted the Jewel Box Revue, a drag show that toured the US for 30 years, spreading its popularity all over the country and inspiring a number of imitators.

Now, thanks to shows like *RuPaul's Drag Race*, these incredible performances are respected and enjoyed by a far wider audience than ever before.

IT'S TIME FOR DRAG QUEEN STORY HOUR

While drag queens still deal with stigma and persecution in some parts of the world today, their growing presence in pop culture has led to greater acceptance.

Drag Queen Story Hour was started in 2015 by San Francisco author Michelle Tea, who wanted an event for children that was more inclusive for LGBTQ+ families. The first one was held in San Francisco's gay-friendly Castro district and featured popular drag performer Honey Mahogany reading stories for kids.

It was a hit, and Drag Queen Story Hour has since spread throughout the world, with more than 40 groups from the US to Germany to Japan, staging local story hours in public libraries and museums. The books chosen are a mix of children's classics as well as stories that deal with LGBTQ+ pride and education.

While there has been some backlash from conservative groups against the concept, it continues to be popular with kids and families looking for a little variety in their story hour.

ROADSIDE
ATTRACTIONS

WOW

THIS WAY

Lucy the Elephant:
A Roadside Behemoth

Placing something eye-catching on the side of a major road is a great way to convince people to stop and spend some money. That was the intention of James V. Lafferty, who, in 1881, built a 65-foot-tall, elephant-shaped real estate office in the quiet beach town of Margate City, New Jersey. He even got a patent for it, securing the exclusive rights to build animal-shaped buildings for 17 years.

The elephant, later named Lucy, had telescopes in its eyes and an open-air deck on its back from which prospective buyers could inspect the real estate plots on offer. People loved Lucy and she actually ended up moving quite a bit of property!

By the 1960s, though, Lucy had fallen into serious disrepair. Local citizens from Margate decided to save her. The 90-ton structure was moved several blocks over, to city-owned land, and completely restored. In 1976, she was named a National Historic Landmark, listed as the oldest still-running roadside attraction in the United States.

Lucy remains in Margate City to this day, having survived the brutal winds and flooding of Hurricane Sandy in 2012. She still hosts more than 100,000 visitors a year and even ran for president in 2016, proving that you can never forget an elephant.

In 2020, Lucy the Elephant became a temporary listing on AirBnB, charging $138 a night for the privilege of staying in a giant elephant.

The Smallest House in Great Britain

Sometime during the 16th century, a house was built in Conwy, Wales. The original builder is lost to history, but we can assume that they were something of a minimalist, as the house was built on less than 57 square feet of land.

Despite its tiny footprint, the Quay House is split into two floors, with the upstairs featuring a bedroom and the downstairs offering up a tiny living room area and fireplace.

It was used through the centuries as a mini-domicile until the year 1900, when a fisherman named Robert Jones became the final occupant. Jones was 6-feet-3 inches tall and couldn't physically stand up straight in his own home.

The local city council decreed that the house could no longer be a home for humans. But Jones still owned the property and passed it down to his kin (which is not exactly what you want to hear at the reading of a will).

Some years later, the Quay House was decreed by the Guinness Book of World Records to be the smallest house in Great Britain, and it became a tourist attraction shortly thereafter. Tours of the tiny house are held daily at a price of £1 for adults, 50 pence for kids. Just mind your head.

The Cabazon Dinosaurs

If you're driving from Los Angeles to Palm Springs, you may see two life-size dinosaurs just chilling on the side of the road. The 65-foot T-Rex and the 150-foot-long Brontosaurus were built by Claude K. Bell, who really wanted people to eat at his Wheel Inn restaurant.

Bell was originally a sculpture artist at a nearby amusement park called Knott's Berry Farm and decided a dinosaur was the perfect way to lure drivers off the highway. His first project was the Brontosaurus (called Dinny), which cost him $300,000 in 1975. It was inspired by a memory from his childhood in Atlantic City, when he saw a house shaped like an elephant (likely Lucy from page 102, since she lives not far from AC!).

Satisfied with his first creation, Bell went on to make his T-Rex in 1986. He had grand plans, seeking to make his creatures have glowing red eyes and spit fire. As he told the Associated Press, he wanted to "scare the dickens out of a lot of people driving up over the pass."

Sadly, Bell died shortly after his T-Rex was finished, and his family sold his famous dinos. You can still visit, but you should know that it's now home to a creationist museum and gift shop that deny evolution. So maybe just appreciate them from afar?

The Mystery Hole: West Virginia

Legend has it that a man named Donald Wilson discovered a "mystery hole" in West Virginia in 1972. Within the hole, the traditional rules of gravity ceased to apply! And, thus, a roadside attraction was born.

To make his Mystery Hole a hit, Wilson built dozens of billboards highlighting the hole's magical properties, proclaiming that "seeing is believing!" Upon arrival, people encountered a large metal shed with a VW Beetle sticking out of it and a gorilla statue at the door. Wilson wisely encouraged visitors not to share what they found within the hole, so as to create even more mystery.

Unfortunately, the suspense could only last so long, and the Mystery Hole closed in 1996, as the shed had fallen into ruin. But, shortly thereafter, a couple from Michigan purchased the land and refurbished the attraction (and its accompanying gift shop) to its 1970s' kitchy heights. They maintain the vow of secrecy and ban photos from being taken within the Hole.

So what, exactly, is in the Hole? It seems unfair to say, but the official Mystery Hole website does make it clear that people with vertigo or heart ailments should not enter. You've been warned.

CENSORED

The Icelandic Phallological Museum

There are museums for dinosaurs, trains, dog collars, and bread. So why not an entire museum dedicated to the penis? Welcome to the Icelandic Phallological Museum, located in Reykjavík.

The museum was created in 1997 by Sigurður Hjartarson. As a child, Hjartarson was given a cattle whip made from a bull's penis, and that sparked a lifelong fascination. Friends would give him penises from various animals as gifts, and nearby whaling stations in Iceland would even donate whale penises for the effort. Eventually, his collection grew to be large enough to be housed in its own museum.

In 2011, speaking to *Salon* about his passion, Hjartarson said that it's never-ending. "Collecting penises is like collecting anything," he said. "You can never stop, you can never catch up, you can always get a new one, a better one." His son has since taken over the business, continuing the bizarre lifelong mission of his father.

And the museum's largest specimen? A 6-foot-long sperm whale penis that is, shockingly, just the tip. The whole thing would be 13 feet long and weigh around 800 pounds. And so the quest continues. After all, there's always a bigger penis to chase.

The Hair Museum of Avanos

In the Cappadocia region of Turkey, there lives a pottery master named Galip Körükçü. He owns his own shop, Chez Galip, where he sells his wares and teaches enthusiastic young pottery fans his art.

Directly below his shop, however, is something else entirely.

Forty years ago, Körükçü received a parting gift from a female friend of his: a lock of her hair. Over the decades, others began to follow suit upon hearing the story, and now his basement is covered with hair samples from more than 16,000 women from all over the world. The hair is taped to the walls alongside handwritten notes detailing the hair's original owner and origin. It's . . . super creepy.

But that hasn't stopped visitors from popping in and donating a few locks to the world's only hair museum. Those who do are in for a treat, however, as Körükçü selects 20 lucky hair donors each year and rewards them with free pottery training at his studio for a week.

Granted, if you win, it'll be hard to convince your friends you aren't traveling to be murdered by a hair-obsessed madman, but none of the reviews seem to mention previous murders, so you're probably good to go.

The Thing: Arizona

Interstate-10 runs across the entire state of Arizona, and for 200 miles of that span, drivers will see something advertised on the side of the road. Well, not *something*. *The* Thing. "What is it?" the signs ask. "It's a sight to behold!" they proclaim.

The so-called "mystery in the desert" arrived in Arizona in 1965. The owner of The Thing, Thomas Binkley Prince, built a small shed to house it and charged 25 cents for a look. Those willing to pay were granted a peek at what appeared to be a mummy with its child, placed inside a glass coffin. A large hat is placed on the mummy's lower region, ensuring modesty.

Thanks to a lack of competition in the middle of the desert, The Thing's popularity increased, and Prince built up the attraction with more ridiculous sights and sounds, like a wooly mammoth foot and a Rolls-Royce supposedly owned by Adolf Hitler.

In 2018, The Thing exhibit was fully revamped to include an intricate backstory involving an ongoing war between aliens and dinosaurs. The Thing, of course, played an important role in the pitched battle, highlighting the real history of our planet.

Oh, and the price for admission has been raised from a quarter to $5.

Nagoro Village

In the 1960s, the town of Nagoro in Japan used to be thriving, thanks to its hydroelectric dam, which brought in jobs and families. Its population was once about 300 people, but now that has dwindled to just 37 residents. And yet Nagoro has become an internationally known attraction, thanks to one woman and her life-size dolls.

Tsukimi Ayano grew up in the town during its heyday but left to go to the big city. When she returned, she realized how much the town's population had moved away and decided to do something about it. She started planting seeds for a garden, but when they didn't grow, she realized that she needed a scarecrow. So she made one herself: a full-size scarecrow, inspired by her father.

Thus began a quest to bring the town back to its former glory by re-creating its former inhabitants in life-size doll form. Many of the dolls include those who have died, while others just look like people who moved away. "I'm very good at making grandmothers," she said in a documentary about her quest, *Valley of the Dolls*.

Ayano's doll count is now over 400, and they're all over the village. They're posed and dressed as if they were performing the tasks they'd be doing if they were still there: electricians, teachers, gardeners. They've since brought living visitors to the town, hoping to get a look at the bizarre and sweet efforts of one woman just trying to bring her village back to life.

Official Center of the World: California

In 1985, a Frenchman living in the US wrote a children's story about a dragon named Coe who discovers that the true "center of the world" is located in a desert town called Felicity, on the southern tip of California. The town didn't exist, but the author, Jacques-André Istel, had been living on 2,600 acres of desolate California land at the time and decided to make his book a reality.

Istel founded the real-life Felicity, California, with his wife in 1986 and was quickly voted the mayor (unanimously, with two votes). As mayor, Istel convinced the local Imperial County Board of Supervisors that, yes, Felicity was indeed the center of the world. The French government's own Institut Géographique National agreed, and thus it was so. (There is no scientific backing for this title and the designation is essentially meaningless, so it's likely that some bureaucrats were having a slow day when the request came in.)

To celebrate his accomplishment, Istel set to work on a 21-foot-tall pyramid made of glass and stone. Directly under the pyramid's point: the Center. Visitors have to pay $3 for the privilege of seeing it, but they are also treated to gorgeous stone plaques of history and art, along with a beautiful chapel that Istel built himself. It's quite a sight.

As for whether his point is actually the Center of the World, Istel admitted to the *New York Times* in 2014 that it's all a bit ridiculous. "The center of the world could be in your pocket!" he said.

The House on the Rock

In Wisconsin, on the top of a massive column of rock, sits a house. It is the grand poobah of all roadside attractions and one of the strangest places on earth.

The House on the Rock was created by eccentric designer Alex Jordan Jr. in 1959. It is best known for its inexplicable collections that fill just about every room and that continue to expand today. One room is lined with antique rifles, another with clocks, another with enormous music machines.

The Whale Room is so called because of a 200-foot-long imaginary sea creature with teeth that is suspended from the ceiling, jumping out of reach of a squid's tentacles.

And then you'll find the Streets of Yesterday, an old-timey, early 1900s town set up within the house itself, complete with fake shops and even a fortune teller.

But the highlight of the House on the Rock is the carousel, an indoor monstrosity with 269 rideable creatures (none of which are horses). It's dotted with 182 chandeliers, and above it all are hundreds of life-size mannequins dressed as angels.

There is truly nothing like the House on the Rock, and there's no better excuse to pull over to the side of the road.

Author Acknowledgments

This book has taken a bit of a winding road to finally arrive in your hands, and it's thanks to many folks for making it happen. I'd first like to thank my wife, Alex, who was incredibly patient and helpful over the course of this project, especially considering she was working to bring our first child into the world for a large chunk of it. She brings light to my life every day and it wouldn't have happened without her.

I'd also like to thank Allegra Frank and Chris Plante, my co-hosts on the podcast, *The History of Fun*, which helped inspire this book. Relatedly, major props to Justin McElroy for his lovely forward and to his wife, Sydnee McElroy.

Their *Sawbones* podcast was a big motivator for me to dive into the world of history.

Thanks, of course, go to Charlie Olsen at Inkwell Management, who more or less saved this book from an abrupt cancellation. And a very special thanks to Jess Riordan, Britny Brooks, and the rest of the team at Running Press for letting us shine a little light on this wacky world of fun.

Lastly, my enormous gratitude to my illustrator, Sonny Ross. They initially brought this project to my attention way back in 2018 and have been unflagging in their commitment to it ever since. Their talent knows no bounds and I'm humbled to share these pages with them.

Illustrator Acknowledgments

I would like to thank Chris Plante and Allegra Frank, and, of course, Russ for agreeing to help make this book when I sent a random message one day. Thank you to the Running Press team for making this happen and to my art director,

Rachel Peckman, for elevating the work to a higher standard. And lastly thank you to my wonderful wife, Sarah, without whom none of this would exist. My constant, my biggest supporter and my best friend to cheer me on throughout.

Index

About the Author

Russ Frushtick is a journalist based in New York City, where he lives with his wife and newborn son. He has been covering the world of video games and technology for over 15 years and was the co-founder of the popular website, Polygon. His writing has been featured in *The New York Times*, New York Magazine's Vulture, The Verge, and Vox. He's also made appearances as an industry expert on BBC News, CNBC, and MTV, among others, and co-hosts a weekly podcast about video games called *The Besties*. He's somewhat color-blind.

About the Illustrator

Sonny Ross is a commercial illustrator based in Manchester, U.K. with their wife Sarah and a small army of pets. Their work mostly includes editorial illustrations for clients such as *The Washington Post*, *The New York Times*, and *The Guardian*, but they have been known to wander off; creating textiles, children's books and painting murals so large they needed a very scary cherry picker to reach the top. In fact, they will likely say yes to any creative endeavor that sounds fun.